MW01248059

The Guide to Our Eternal Destiny:
God's Preserved Inerrant Word or Text Preferences of Scholars?

A Christian View of Textual Criticism and Modern Translation Practice

by
Dr. Larry Bednar, Textual Consultant

William Carey Bible Society

King James Bible Research Council

Accelerated Baptist Missions Institutes
www.AcceleratedBaptistMissionsInstitute.com

> Emphasizing translation of the Received Text of the KJB that world people groups may have God's Word in their languages

Scripture Texts of Modern Textual Critics and Translators Are Based on Scholar Preferences to a Large Degree

Textual critics deny preservation of the scripture text, saying all manuscripts show accidental copyist error. They define error by opinion and suggest original text content can be restored well enough through their text preferences, resulting in opinion-guided critical texts that are the basis of most modern versions. They reject our traditional Greek text and favor a type derived from manuscripts lost to churches for ~1500 years and marked by evidence of tampering, resulting in translations that at times depart from traditional-text support of doctrines like the deity of Jesus, salvation by grace and believer's baptism. They disregard all this, saying they seek to decide what the original writers meant to say, as if they could know the minds of original writers, or actually, the mind of the Holy Spirit who inspired and endowed the text.

The Bible-believer viewpoint

God's preservation of the text is the only means to ensure that we have His Word, and a preserved text possessed by His people over the centuries can only be a traditional one. True biblical scholarship reveals God's preservation of His Word by traditional texts, and rejects the notion that accuracy depends on tinkering and text-preferences of scholars. It classifies texts by theological, doctrinal and textual standards of excellence expected of the text that God preserves, and rejects those not meeting this standard. The present treatise contrasts quality of traditional texts with that of texts produced by the exercise of scholar opinion.

A true text of God's Word will exhibit consistent accuracy indicative of inerrancy historically preserved by His hand, from autograph originals, to select copies, to select translations. And it will exhibit evidence of His hand by inspiratonas the means of inerrancy preservation. Such study of a text tells us if it's an end-product of inspired inerrant autographs, and traditional texts, including the KJB, prove to be true autograph representatives, but critical texts and modern English versions don't qualify.

Comparing English Bible Translations

Modern versions reflecting scholar opinion and text preferences present a danger of losing God's preserved Word, as we see by comparing them with our traditional English Bible. We contrast theological, doctrinal and textual quality of the KJB with that of the NIV and NASV mainly and also the NKJV, NRSV and RSV.

Evidence of tampering in Greek texts favored by scholars
<u>1</u>. Acts 8:36-38. The baptism of the Ethiopian eunuch
KJB

36: *...here is water; what doth hinder me to be baptized?*

37: *And Philip said, <u>if thou believest</u> with all thine heart, <u>thou mayest</u>. And he...said, <u>I believe</u> that Jesus Christ is the Son of God.*

38: *...they went down both into the water...and he baptized him.*

NIV

36:*..the eunuch said, "Look here is water. Why shouldn't I be baptized?"*

37:

38: *And he gave orders to stop the chariot. Then both Philip and the eunuch went down into the water and Philip baptized him.*

The KJB 8:37 forbids baptism of all not believing in Jesus Christ as God's Son. With this verse missing in the NIV critical Greek text, all persons are candidates for baptism, regardless of their beliefs. Some readers may conclude baptism, not belief, is the crucial thing, a popular modern concept. They may never see the need for conversion through true belief in God's Son.

Critics favor short readings and see no omission in their text, and the subject verse isn't in most Greek manuscripts, so they think their case here is strong. But the NIV Greek-text verse 37 on the eunuch's confession has been omitted, as the NIV shows. Evidence of tampering is strong, for in the absence of the verse Philip doesn't answer the eunuch's question on what hindered his baptism, and the confession of Jesus as God's Son refutes early

3

Cerinthian-type gnostics who said Jesus had a human father, and were famous for producing their own strange scripture versions.

The verse in question is in 6th-century Greek manuscripts, scripture quotes by church elders and the Old Latin Bible. God's Old Latin text, preserved in Dark-Ages history, shows the verse was in the Traditional Text of early western biblical churches.

Critics who "restore" the text have trouble identifying sound doctrine in a matter related to salvation and Jesus' deity. We may wonder how prevalent such problems are in their Greek texts.

2. Lk.2:14 Exclusive salvation? The KJB and its Greek Received Text say of the First Advent, *Glory to God in the highest, and on earth peace, good will toward men.* Critics favor the Alexandrian, peace to *men of good will* that the NIV renders *men on whom his favor rests*, suggesting the Gnostic notion of exclusive salvation. The peace is God's salvation offer by God's grace to *whosoever will* (Rev.22:17), not just select ones of good will or in special favor. The difference is due to *good will* being in the Greek nominative case in the Received Text and the genitive case in the critical. The genitive requires *of*, resulting in a critical-text, <u>men of good will</u> indicative of salvation exclusivity contradicting Rev.22:17. Proper genitive use would be, <u>*peace of* God's good will to men</u>, which is equivalent to the KJB wording.

3. Mark 10:24 A hard way to get to heaven?
KJB...*Jesus answereth again...Children, how hard it is <u>for them that trust in riches</u> to enter into the kingdom of God...*
NIV...*"Children, how hard it is to enter the kingdom of God...*

The KJB says trust in riches hinders trust in Christ for salvation. The NIV hard way indicates works salvation, and Gnostics taught various works-salvation tenets. Now the KJB agrees with nearly all extant manuscripts, but the NIV with only four. Critics say a works-salvation reading is the true harsh one preserved in just four manuscripts, while all others supposedly were altered by conservative scribes who disliked the harsh one, despite likely scarcity of copyists in historically-small biblical churches and a likely abundance of them in historically-large unbiblical churches.

<u>4.</u> Eph.4:6 A Greek text for all who favor universal salvation

KJB: *One God and Father of all, who is above all, and through all, and <u>in you all</u>.*

NASV: *One God and Father of all who is over all and through all and <u>in all</u>.*

Paul speaks to Ephesian Christians in saying God is *in <u>you</u> all*. The NASV critical Greek-text omission of *you* suggests God is in everyone, not just saved persons, and text critics offering such a reading support universal salvation, suggesting readers need not be concerned about conversion crucial to biblical salvation.

Criticizing Textual (Lower) Criticism

Textual critics seem to have trouble discerning truth in a matter as vital as salvation, which should motivate us to look at methods by which they "restore the original text."

A look at textual-criticism methods

Eclecticism: All manuscripts are supposedly consulted, and the readings are decided through scholar opinion. But the Greek text-type underlying the KJB (~94% of all manuscripts) is virtually ignored, and the type called Alexandrian (~4% of manuscripts) is made the main basis of critical texts. A critical text is formed by scholar selection among manuscripts and has never in history existed as a single text representing autograph originals.

Stemmatics: Genealogical relationships of manuscripts, placing them in families, have supposedly been identified, but families mix and confuse, and one can never arrive at a single archetype approximating an autograph. The futility of the method is seen in that a family called the Caesarean, is now thought to be just a mixture of other families, not a separate one, and one called the Western is now suspected of being of similar nature.

Cladistics: This approach, borrowed from biological evolutionist notions, assumes text-types form a series of related branches of development. The result is a lot of branches with no autograph trunk. Even if branches did point to one archetype, this might be just an early singular case of deviation from the autographs.

Copy Text Editing: In this approach, popularized by Westcott and Hort, a master manuscript is selected and adjusted through others. The Alexandrian Vaticanus was selected as a master copy and other Alexandrians (~4% of all manuscripts) were consulted to arrive at a "best" text. Today theories of text history preferring the Alexandrian Text, are known to be faulty, yet scholars still promote a presumed superiority of the Alexandrian-type text.

Some specific tenets of textual criticism

Textual criticism is a subjective biased practice, as seen from the tenets scholars adopt to establish original readings. These ensure preference for Alexandrian-type manuscripts underlying modern critical texts, just because scholars think these are the best.

For example, text critics presume any text changes are due to conservative scribes making difficult readings smoother, longer and more orthodox. Thus orthodoxy and clarity of expression are made suspect, and a well-known tendency for short Alexandrian readings is artificially preferred. But short readings result from tampering by those eliminating teachings they dislike. Heretics disagreeing with Christian doctrine were known to alter texts during early manuscript copying.[1] How can scholars ignore high tampering potential in Alexandrian manuscripts showing evidence of text shortening in support of heresies prominent at times and locales associated with these manuscripts? How can they insist conservative scribes altered God's Word to suit themselves? And how in the world do they justify pre-determined suspicion of orthodoxy and clarity of expression? Indeed suggest original readings are difficult and apt to be simplified by conservatives,

[1.] Colwell, E.C. 1952. *What is the Best N. T.?* U. of Chicago Press, p53.

ignores the expectation of simplistic readings in the text provided through the auspices of God, who should want His will plainly known. To say conservatives simplified scripture is to say that simplicity of expression is to be suspect and scrutinized, causing endless uncertainty. Difficult readings easily arise due to limited intelligence of those at work in tampering, and difficulty involved in trying to make tampering look like part of a true text.

Another tenet guaranteeing Alexandrian-reading preference stipulates that oldest readings are preferred, for Alexandrians have long been accepted by scholars as the oldest. But the age tenet isn't followed with recent finds of non-Alexandrian readings in papyri older than Alexandrian manuscripts,[2] indicating the tenet is followed only if it supports Alexandrian manuscripts.

A tenet stipulating bald preference for Alexandrian readings, is the most blatant of biased tenets ensuring preference of them. Alexandrian-text readings are presumed to be closer to original readings than others just because scholars believe this.

Another tenet stipulates a reading that best explains the origin of others is preferred. This favors a manuscript with some variance that initiates a series of manuscripts with progressive variance. Such a series can never be associated with providential preservation, only with copyist error or tampering, and judgment on which reading is correct is subjective. Efforts to identify a true reading by this tenet are flawed, for truth to one critic is just error to another, and justifying of opinion is the likely result.

Selection and application of tenets is based on opinion, so it's no surprise to find that tenets usually don't agree enough to support a given reading. Thus more opinion is exercised to decide which subjectively-derived tenet takes precedence. Unsurprisingly, lack of consistent results shows that the tenets are inadequate to derive original readings. Failure of the process is clear in that critics at times ignore predominant evidence from their own preferred type

2. Sturz, H.A. 1984. *The Byzantine Text Type & New Testament Textual Criticism.* N.Y. T. Nelson. p53-95. Sturz supports Alexandrian texts.

of manuscripts and choose entirely on the basis of opinion. The process of textual criticism is incredibly subjective and varies from one scholar to another. How can mere men decide what is or isn't God's Word? There's no objectivity in any of this and no consideration of God's role in preserving His Word for us.[3]

Westcott & Hort: These influential 19th-century critics treated the sacred text the same as secular literature. Hort said, "For ourselves, we dare not introduce considerations which could not reasonably be applied to other ancient texts, supposing them to have documentary attestation of equal amount, variety and antiquity." They had a low view of text quality, yet denied deliberate tampering, saying, "Even among the numerous unquestionably spurious readings of the New Testament, there are no signs of deliberate falsification of the text for dogmatic purposes." [4]

Error in Alexandrian-Based Critical Texts

Evidence of deliberate falsification for dogmatic purposes: We evaluate this denial of deliberate falsification as we consider ancient heresy. Doctrinal and textual error we've seen, including evidence of Gnostic tampering, is plain in the Alexandrian text of Westcott and Hort and associated critical Greek texts. Gnostic and Arian heresies were troublesome in churches of the early centuries, and were centered at Alexandria in Egypt, the main locale associated with the Alexandrian-type text.

---

3. Ewert shows how unreliable judgment of critics can be, even when they favor a true reading, as at 1 Cor.15:51 where Paul says, *We shall not all sleep, but we shall all be changed*. Ewert says this is a true, but difficult, reading, for Paul died. But Paul didn't say he or his peers wouldn't die. He spoke of those alive at the Rapture, for *we* is the church of all ages. The reading is logical and genuine, and saying it explains the origin of a series of related distorted readings in other texts is misleading, suggesting the true reading began corruptions seen in other texts (Ewert, D. *From Ancient Tablets to Modern Translations*. Grand Rapids. Zondervan. p160).
4. *The N. T. in the Orig. Greek*. Vol 2. Lond. MacMillan. 1881. p277-82

5. John 1:18 Only begotten Son or only begotten God?

KJB: *No man hath seen God at any time; the only* <u>*begotten Son,*</u> *which is in the bosom of the Father, he hath declared him.*

NASV: *No man has seen God at any time; the only* <u>*begotten God,*</u> *who is in the bosom of the Father, He has explained Him.*

NIV: *No one has ever seen God, but God the One and Only, who is at the Father's side, has made him known.*

The KJB Greek text says Jesus is God's Begotten Son in the bosom of, very close to, the Father. Eternal Christ had no beginning of days, becoming the Begotten Son of God at His Incarnation when He entered the stream of human events in a body. His body was generated by the Holy Ghost, so He was the Son of God, and it was generated through Mary, so He was also the Son of Man.

Begotten God of Critical Greek texts reflects an Arian notion that Christ was a lesser god begotten/created by the Father in eternity past. *Begotten God, who is in the bosom of the Father* suggests Christ begotten as god in the Father's bosom of creation. There's no such entity as *begotten God*, for true God has no beginning of days. Arianism arose in Alexandria, Egypt in the 4th century, and manuscripts with "God" in the text are 4th-century Alexandrians.

Yet scholars say the NASV attests Christ's deity better than the KJB in using "God" for *Son*, but the effect is the opposite, attacking His deity with error indicative of an ancient heresy. If Christ were begotten in any sense other than by the Incarnation in human form, He would be begotten as god, and would be a created god. The KJB has no shadow of such a problem.

The NIV omits *begotten* due to its Critical Greek-text *God*, making "God the One and Only" stand at His own side declaring Himself. This is due to commitment to a faulty Greek text.

The NRSV *No one has ever seen God. It is God the only Son, who is close to the Father's heart, who has made him known* is like the KJB Greek text in meaning. But it changes critical-text language notably, paraphrasing to remove *begotten* and retain

God. Critical-text commitment is indicated, but in making this text more realistic, the committee refutes its presumed accuracy. They seem willfully bound to it, despite the error. And their *God the only Son* contradicts Job 38:7 that calls angels sons of God.

<u>6.</u> 1 Tim. 3:16 Some slight of hand

KJV...*great is the mystery of godliness:* <u>*God*</u> *was manifest in the flesh, justified in the spirit, seen of angels, preached unto the gentiles, believed on in the world, received up into glory.*

NASV...*great is the mystery of godliness:* <u>*He who*</u> *was revealed in the flesh, Was vindicated in the Spirit, Beheld by angels…*

In the KJB, Jesus in His earthly history is *God…in the flesh*, but the NASV Greek text has *who* for *God*. *Theos* (God) is easily made *os* (who) by dropping *The* and adding a vowel breathing mark. Awkward language results, and some manuscripts have *which*, adding to a sense of tampering. The NASV suggests Jesus was part of *the mystery of godliness*, or how God works in <u>men</u>. The NIV says *He appeared in a body*, and *He* can be a mere man, for any man is a personality appearing in a body, so testimony to Jesus' deity is lost. NIV translators attempted a correction by omitting *who* or *which*, but accentuated the error by poor language arising from trying to justify a corrupt Greek text. Tampering would be due to Cerinthian-type Gnostics who suggested that Christ appeared in the flesh of a mere man Jesus.

<u>7.</u> Luke 2:33 Joseph is not the father of Jesus!

KJB: *And <u>Joseph and his mother</u> marvelled at those things which were spoken of him* (spoken by Simeon of Christ).

NASV: *And his <u>father and mother</u> were amazed at the things…*

NIV: *The child's <u>father and mother</u> marveled at what was said...*

In Lk.2:33 critical Greek texts call Joseph Jesus' father, denying Jesus' deity. But Joseph was just a foster-father, the Holy Ghost being the true father of Christ's earthly form. The error derives from Alexandrian manuscripts said by scholars to be the best, but tampering by Cerinthian-type Gnostics is indicated. They denied Jesus was deity in the flesh, saying He was born of a human father. They suggested He had a temporary deity through union with the divine Logos at the baptism in Jordan, and they believed the divine nature vanished on the cross where Jesus supposedly died a mere man.

Now if a mere man died for our sins at Calvary, Christians are unforgiven. And getting used to passages like this will rob us of the sense of divine mission and purpose, consecration to the work and related hardships on behalf of a mere blessed man not being very appealing. This problem, that doesn't trouble critics, is unique to texts of a few manuscripts derived from Alexandria, Egypt in the 4th century A.D. Gnostic heresy developed there in the 2nd - 3rd centuries, and carryover of associated error in 4th-century manuscripts could be expected.

Critics consider these arguments invalid, saying that in Lk.2:48 the KJB and its Greek text refer to Joseph as Jesus' father, but they miss the point. In Lk.2:48, Mary, a human being speaking carelessly, calls Joseph Jesus' father when she's displeased that Jesus absented Himself from the family company. Scripture is inerrant, but in being so, it records human error, including that of Mary. Indeed in the KJB Lk.2:49, immediately after Mary's statement, the Lord instructs us in this matter as He corrects Mary to remind her who His Father really is, saying... *Wist ye not that I must be about <u>my Father's</u> business?* (business of heaven). This gives a reader proper teaching on human error.

The problem in modern critical texts is that the speaker in Lk.2:33 isn't a person speaking improperly. The speaker is the authoritative inerrant voice of the Gospel, or in effect, the Holy Ghost who inspired the Gospel. It's not credible to imagine that He who is the inerrant voice of the Gospel, and the true Father of Christ's earthly form, would call Joseph the father of Jesus. But a Gnostic tampering at Luke 2 could see the advantage of altering verse 33 to suit his dogma and the futility of altering verse 48.

Modern critics accept manuscript language that improperly refers to Jesus' earthly family. A proper term in referring to Mary and Joseph collectively would be "parents of Jesus," for together they performed all parental responsibilities after Jesus' birth. Joseph is a parent in the sense of a foster-father who exercises authority and ongoing functions of a parent after the birth. Thus scripture use of *parents* for a mother and foster-father collectively doesn't attack Christ's deity. But to suggest scripture calling Joseph the father of Jesus is totally unacceptable.

<u>8</u>. Philip.2:6,7 Translation error aggravated by text criticism

KJB: *Who being in the form of God thought it not <u>robbery</u> to be equal with God…and took upon him the form of a servant…*

NASV: *who, although He existed in the form of God, did not regard equality with god a thing to be <u>grasped</u> but emptied Himself, taking the form of a bond servant…*

NIV: *Who being in very nature God, did not consider equality with God something to be <u>grasped</u>…*

This isn't a critical-text problem, but relates to that in Lk.2:33. The KJB says Christ in earthly form was God, so equating Himself with God wasn't robbery, as it would be for a mere man. The NIV says Jesus didn't grasp equality with God. "Grasp" is ambiguous, but is wrong in any sense. As "understood," it means Jesus didn't understand Himself as equal with God. As "obtain," it means He didn't consider equality with God something He could obtain. As "retain," it means He once had equality with God, but considered it a thing He couldn't retain, which supports Cerinthianism. This, with Lk.2:33 in modern versions, presents a full range of Cerinthian dogma about Jesus. In Lk.2:33 He is supposedly born of a human father, and in Philippians, His deity can be seen as temporary and thus imposed.

The Greek rare noun *harpagmos* refers to the <u>act</u> of robbing and that type of grasping, not <u>a thing</u> grasped. The noun relates to the verb *harpazo* (to rob), and depicts a seizing in robbery.

"Grasped" in a "retained" sense suggests Jesus gave up equality with God, or gave up His deity, as in Cerinthianism. He gave up privileges as deity (He did Creator works). The Greek text has *harpagmos*, and us of *a thing to be grasped* requires *harpagma*.[5] The altered word choice and syntax are popular in liberal-leaning lexicons, but are inapplicable, for they support Cerinthian dogma. The problem isn't in critical texts, so why do modern translators support Cerinthianism here?

9. 1 John 4:2,3 Tampering that identifies the guilty sect
Docetists claimed Jesus was a phantom spirit who only seemed to have a body, denying deity in the flesh. John says they are of antichrist in the KJB, but the NIV Greek text deviates.

KJB...*Every spirit that confesseth that Jesus Christ is come in the flesh is of God: And every spirit that confesseth not that Jesus Christ is come in the flesh is not of God: and this is that spirit of antichrist.*

NIV...*Every spirit that acknowledges that Jesus Christ has come in the flesh is from God, but every spirit that does not acknowledge Jesus is not from God. This is the spirit of the antichrist...*

The KJB and NIV Greek texts say God ordains spirits that say Jesus *Christ* (God) *is come in the flesh.* But only the KJB Greek says spirits not confessing this are of the antichrist. The NIV *not acknowledge Jesus* (liberals acknowledge the man) is far short of *confesseth not that Jesus Christ is come in the flesh.* In the NIV Greek text, Docetist error is intact, so they didn't tamper here. Cerinthians said Christ came in the flesh of a man, which is close enough to the initial part of the passage that they wouldn't be troubled by it, the tenor being positive. But the latter part exposes their error in rejecting Jesus as God in flesh. Retained Docetist error and deleted Cerinthian error indicates the type of sect guilty of selective tampering here, but modern critics miss this, blindly favoring shorter readings.

5. Jamieson, Fausset & Brown Co. 1997. Hendrickson. Vol.3. p429

10. Lk.24:51,52 A very strange manuscript source
KJB...*he was parted from them, and <u>carried up into heaven</u>. And <u>they worshipped him</u> and returned to Jerusalem with great joy...*
NASV: *And it came about that while he was blessing them, He parted from them. And they returned to Jerusalem with great joy.*

In the KJB, the Savior is worshipped and ascends to heaven. Cerinthians, who said Jesus lost His divine nature at the Cross, wouldn't like His being resurrected, worshipped and ascending bodily to heaven. The NASV follows non-traditional manuscripts that omit <u>all</u> attestation to Jesus' deity, which is obvious tampering of major importance. The KJB presents a triumph of worship of the resurrected divine Christ at the Ascension. The NASV suggests a mere happy parting of earthly friends who had a joyful time together. With this change, the NASV chapter can be understood in terms of a blessed man Jesus who, though raised from the dead by God, wasn't deity, as Cerinthians taught.

Critics eventually rejected this odd rendering. Manuscripts utilized here aren't in the group they normally prefer, so why did they depart from their preferred manuscripts to adopt this rendering that removes all attestation of Jesus' deity in the passage?

11. Various cases of tampering by heretics and others
Ephesians 3:9
KJB: *And to make all men see what is the <u>fellowship</u> of the mystery, which from the beginning of the <u>world</u> hath been hid in God, who created all things <u>by Jesus Christ</u>:*
NASV...*what is the <u>administration</u> of the mystery which for <u>ages</u> has been hidden in God, who created all things___?___*
NIV...*the <u>administration</u> of this mystery, which for <u>ages</u> past was kept hidden in God, who created all things___?___*

Critics favor Alexandrian manuscripts lacking *by Jesus Christ* and deny omission, but gnostics denying Jesus' deity were active in church history when and where Alexandrian texts originated.

14

1. In critical Greek texts *Administration* substitutes for *fellowship*. *Administration* has by far the most manuscript support, but *fellowship* provides the true sense. The text teaches the sharing (fellowship) of a mystery, Gentiles being included so that all the church proclaims a former mystery, the gospel of Creator Christ dying for our sin. *To make all men see* refers to *fellowship* of the mystery, declaring the gospel, and in verses 6-10 Gentiles share in the fellowship. Thus a true reading is restored by Providential intervention when the Received Text supersedes the Traditional (preservation isn't left to sinners). The true *fellowship* replaces faulty *administration*, and a true *by Jesus Christ* is retained.

Ages (Gr. *aion*) and *administration* (Gr. *oikonomia*) relate to each other and seem valid, but linking them supports a gnostic view rejecting Jesus as God, seeing Him as of the *aionon*, lesser deities emanating from a superior God. The critical-text Eph.3:9 can be crudely interpreted as, to *bring to light administration of hidden mystery originating from the aionon in God*. Removing Christ Jesus' creation role and relating *administration* to *aion* supports a gnostic view of themselves as exclusive administrators of mystery knowledge. The KJB *fellowship* makes the true mystery non-exclusive and isolates *aionon* to its usual *ages*. And the KJB removes all hint of error with, *from the beginning of the world*, in lieu of, *from ages past* (either is fine, but KJB translators seem aware of Gnostic text corruption). True readings lost in many manuscripts of a large unbiblical Greek church careless over Gnostic heresy, endured in those of a small biblical church. Variant manuscript support likely reflects relative church size and the number of copyists. True readings were restored in the Received Text to extend truth, for God ensures preservation of the true text revealing Christ as Creator. Scholars imagine Received-Text error, but contrary to them, the Greek terms aren't close enough in spelling to attribute the difference to misreading (koinonia - *fellowship* & oikonomia - *administration*).

2. The Received-Text Col.1:14 *redemption through his blood*, and Acts 8:37 confession of Jesus as God's Son are absent in

most manuscripts. Cerinthians saw Jesus as a mere man indwelled by a Christ who departed at the Cross. To them Jesus was not God's Son so that His blood shed at the Cross, seen as that of a mere man, could not atone for sin. Removing Acts 8:37 and pertinent Col.1:14 wording would serve their dogma.

3. In Rev.22:19 *tree of life* (much manuscript support) reads *book of life* (little support) in the Received Text, restoring original emphasis on loss of names in the *book of life* and death in the lake of fire (Rev.19:15) for subtracting from God's Word. This warns against text-shortening, a notable Cerinthian habit. Loss of right to the tree would seem far less threatening to such heretics.

4. The Received-Text Eph.1:18, *eyes of your <u>understanding</u>* (minor support) restores truth lost with *eyes of your <u>heart</u>* (major support). Gnostics saw good and evil as due to two gods of equal power, so evil seemed inevitable. <u>Heart</u> anguish over inevitable evil and hurt in life leads to pessimism and accepting error like Gnostic "hidden knowledge." Manuscripts *with <u>understanding</u>* in the text hinder Gnostic theology due to emphasis on <u>*mind*</u> that <u>sees</u> truth, for the passage discusses knowing Christ's truth, and the <u>mind</u> can accept in Him harsh truth that the <u>heart</u> can't.

5. Tampering by legalists objecting to forgiveness for adultery is defeated in the Received-Text John 7:53-8:11 that restores lost truth. Many post-4th-century manuscripts have the verse, so this truth wasn't lost for long, and was rightly emphasized anew.

<u>12</u>. John 5:2-7 – Textual critics ignore an obvious omission

5:2 *Now there is in Jerusalem near the sheep gate a pool which in Aramaic* [6] *is called Bethesda...*

5:3 *Here a great number of disabled people used to lie...*

5:4

5:5 *One who was there had been an invalid for 38 years.*

---

6. The text says *Hebrew*, not *Aramaic*. In N.T. times Hebrews commonly spoke Aramaic, but Hebrew language applied to matters of faith. Studies suggest that *Bethesda* is Hebrew and *Bethzatha* is the Aramaic equivalent (Hodges, Z.C. *The Greek Text of the KJV.* "Which Bible." p29.

5:6 *When Jesus saw him lying there and learned that he had been in this condition for a long time, He asked him, "Do you want to get well?"*

5:7 *"Sir," the invalid replied, "I have no one to help me into the pool when the water is stirred. While I am trying to get in, someone else goes down ahead of me."*

Verse 4 absence in the NIV critical Greek text obscures passage sense. Why did the man need to get in the pool, and to do so before others, and why was stirring of the water important?

The KJB verse 4 answers the questions. It says, *For an angel went down at a certain season into the pool, and troubled the water: whosoever then first after the troubling of the water stepped in was made whole of whatsoever disease* (dis - ease) *he had.* This explains the need for pool stirring and to enter it first.

Scholars reject this, despite its solution to the problem and despite its presence in most Greek manuscripts. They claim the true verse is lost, for manuscripts they favor lack it.[7] And they reject it since the 2nd-century church didn't find the miraculous pool,[8] but it would pass away as New Testament healing focused on Christ, and the passage itself marks this change.

13. Mk.16:9-20 An incomplete Gospel?
And they...fled from the sepulchre...neither said they any thing to any man; for they were afraid.

Some say Mark's Gospel ends on this note of fear, the last 12 KJB verses supposedly being unauthentic, even though that content is in other gospels. Supposedly Mark omits the report of Mary Magdalene to disciples, the Emmaus road meeting with Jesus, the great commission and the Ascension. Others claim a lost true

7. White, *The King James Only Controversy.* p156, feels a need to include such a verse could make a scribe add it, so he expects poor language in his favored Greek text. He stresses error of adding to the text and objects to speaking of deletion here, despite indicated deletion in the NIV.
8. Hills, E.F. 1988. *The King James Version Defended.* p145

ending different from that of the KJB.[9]

Such theories arise since a Latin and two Alexandrian manuscripts and a Syriac version omit the 12 verses. But they're in many Greek and Latin manuscripts, versions and quotes, and the Latin manuscript omitting them shows evidence of Docetist tampering. Scholars support their view by manuscript preference and imaginative arguments on a writing style of the 12 verses said to be different from that of Mark.

14. Mk.1:2-3 Illogical grammar of textual critics

KJB: *As it is written in the prophets, Behold I send my messenger before thy face, which shall prepare thy way before thee. The voice of one crying in the wilderness, Prepare ye the way of the Lord, make his paths straight.*

NIV: *It is written in Isaiah the prophet: "I will send my messenger ahead of you, who will prepare your way"...A voice of one calling in the desert, Prepare the way for the Lord, make straight paths for Him.*

The critical Greek-text reading is erroneous, for this reference to John the Baptist is partly in Mal.3:1 and partly in Isa.40:3, so *the prophets* in the Received Text is the true reading. But critics still favor their Greek text, despite its error. They assume that, in assigning the words of two prophets to just one, modern versions are correct since this is the reading of the Greek text they assume is best. But this is what must be proved and can't be assumed.

They invent a theory to support their opinion, saying New Testament quotes of the Old Testament tend to reference only a

9. White, p256, suggests error in the 12 verses, such as Jesus appearing in another form in 16:12, saying this denies a physical resurrected body, but it was a supernatural body (Lk.24:33-40). He notes 11 disciples in 16:14 (no Thomas makes 10), but the 11 were the Jn.20:26 group with Thomas. He says Jesus wouldn't likely rebuke disciples for unbelief in their fearful post-Crucifixion state, but He did just that earlier when they were fearful (Mt.8:26). Speculation can't discredit scripture.

major prophet who gave the passage, ignoring a contributor of lesser stature. But part of the Mark passage is only in Malachi and part only in Isaiah, and by eliminating reference to Malachi, the NIV has Isaiah speaking Malachi's quote.

Further, Mark tells of John's mission from the perspective of God the Father, Malachi from that of Christ and Isaiah from that of John. All three perspectives are involved in the interpretation.

An early copyist could create this error since similar quotes in Mt.3:3 and Lk.3:4 note only Isaiah's part, but a copyist who attributes to Isaiah what Malachi wrote is in error. Each gospel writer references different parts of the Isaiah/Malachi texts for the purposes of his account. Each has his own purpose, as we see in that Luke continues the Isaiah quote with more content from Isa.40:4-5, while Mark and Matthew do not.

Scholars would "correct" supposed New Testament error by attributing to Isaiah what Malachi said. They even try to justify this, saying the New Testament may ignore prophets of lesser stature and favor those of greater, but God allows no respect of persons, so their effort to justify poor language is compounded by their unsound claim. They cite Mt.27:9 on the potter's field and 30 pieces of silver in Judas' betrayal as illustrating their claim. They assume Jeremiah gives part of the Matthew quote, and Zechariah the most, only Jeremiah being named due to his greater status. But no Mt.27:9 tie to the Jeremiah book exists (see Jer.32:6-15, 18:2-3 offered by scholars, but *potter* and *field* refer to different matters here, and the field in Jer.32 sells for 17 shekels (weight) of silver, which isn't likely the same as 30 pieces (number). And Matthew's words have no syntactical likeness to those of Zechariah. Matthew didn't <u>quote</u> Zechariah or Jeremiah, evidently quoting what Jeremiah <u>spoke</u> orally for recording in non-canonical writing later canonized in the New Testament. The KJB rendering is the only logical inerrant one.

Some textual critics eventually reject their own dogma
Westcott and Hort theory eventually disgusted some supporters.

1. J. Rendel Harris: He said the New Testament text wasn't settled, calling it, *more than ever, and perhaps finally, unsettled.*[10]
2. J.R. Harris also said all manuscripts, including Vaticanus and Sinaiticus, *were actually reeking with dogmatic falsifications.*[11]
3. Kirsopp Lake: *In spite of the claims of Westcott and Hort and Von Soden, we do not know the original form of the gospels, and it is quite likely that we never shall.*[12]
4. F.C. Conybeare. *The ultimate text, if there ever was one that deserves to be so called, is forever irrecoverable.*[13]

Effects of Modern Translation Practice on Text Accuracy

Modern translators add to problems of text-critic error. We begin with teachings on human nature and then address various others.

1. 1 Cor.9:27 Abusing our bodies?

KJB: *But I keep under my body, and bring it into subjection…*

NIV: *…I beat my body and make it my slave…*

The KJB tells of keeping bodily desires under control, a crucial part of Christian witness. The NIV teaches unbiblical beating of Paul's body, a temple of the Holy Spirit. An overly specific sense of the Greek, not applicable in this context, is used in the NIV.

2. Mt.23:24 KJB Distinguishing of great and small matters

To scholars this KJB rendering, that Pharisees and scribes *strain at a gnat and swallow a camel*, should say *strain out.*[14,15] Grammar indicates *strain out*, but metaphoric context alters word sense. *Swall-*

10. Harris, J.R. *Side Lights on New Testament Research.* London. James Clarke & Co. 1908. p3
11. Harris R. *Bulletin of the Bezan Club.* Nov. 1926. p5
12. Lake, K. & S. Family 13 (Ferrar). Phil. U. of PA Press. 1941. pV11
13. Conybeare, F.C. *History of New Testament Criticism.* London. Watts & Co.1910. p129
14. Scrivener, F.H.A. 1873. ed. Cambridge Paragraph Bible.
15. Ewert, D. 1983. *From Ancient Tablets to Modern Trans.* Zond. p202

ow a camel signifies easily accepting great error, as in *swallow a huge lie*, and *strain at a gnat* signifies great effort in judging trivial issues. Pharisees and scribes didn't separate (strain out) trivial issues from big ones, but ignored (swallowed) great error to fuss over (strain at) the trivial. Context applies the major sense that Pharisees and scribes strain-at their goal to strain-out of other's lives what to them is great error, but is gnat-like in importance. This is expressed best by *strain at* that avoids adding unnecessary words to the text.

Modern critics and translators seem confused over what scripture says about human nature and context importance. Let's see how well translators do with doctrine that is basic to scripture.

<u>3</u>. 1 Cor.1:18. Saved or always being saved?
KJB...*the preaching of the cross is to them that perish foolishness; but unto us which <u>are saved</u> it is the power of God.*
NIV...*the message of the cross is foolishness to those who are perishing, but to us who <u>are being saved</u> it is the power of God.*

The KJB *are saved* indicates a present-tense salvation due to a past-tense experience. But the NIV *are being saved* suggests an ongoing salvation process instead of a complete one. A works-salvationist will relate to this in his endless works for salvation.

NIV translators used the continuous sense of a Greek present passive participle instead of a present-tense verb. Either is right grammatically, but the translators used the participle since that reflects their Greek text. But Greek grammar doesn't perfectly match the English, and at times context calls for a verb change. The present-tense verb is best to avoid a wrong English sense.

Scholars say salvation doesn't have only a past-tense aspect, and there is a future-tense aspect in that one day we'll have our salvation finalized on deliverance unto the Savior and away from sin and corruption of this world. But some scholars follow Greek grammar to the extent of suggesting the Greek participle signifies individuals being saved in an ongoing process.[16] This isn't true,

21

except for possible brief delay from first belief to assurance. It's sanctification, not salvation, that's ongoing, so *are saved* is best. Using the English participle causes poor interpretation, suggesting an ever-incomplete process of salvation in individuals, due to verb mismatch. If the Greek is used, corrective English is needed to speak of salvation that is ongoing only in the sense that new souls are being saved. Translators must be able to handle such potential problems, as those of the KJB clearly were.

<u>4</u>. 1 Jn.2:29 Are we made righteous by doing what is right?

> KJB...*let no man deceive you: he that <u>doeth righteousness</u> is righteous even as he* (Christ) *is righteous.*
>
> NIV ...*do not let anyone lead you astray. He who <u>does what is right</u> is righteous, just as he is righteous*...

A works-salvationist will appreciate this NIV translation of the critical text allowing poor interpretation (a wrong Greek-noun sense). The NIV says doing right, good works that many unsaved people do, make one as righteous as Jesus Christ. But, as in the KJB, Christ's righteousness in a believer by the Spirit given in salvation is what makes him righteous, which is by grace, not works.

<u>5</u>. Luke 21:19 Does standing firm impart salvation?

> KJB: *In your patience <u>possess</u> ye your souls.*
> NIV: *By standing firm you will <u>gain</u> life.*
> NRSV *By your endurance you will <u>gain</u> your souls.*

In Lk.21:19 the Greek can suggest life, salvation, is gained by standing firm in trials (works salvation). The Greek verb sense varies, so

<u>16</u>. White, p133 defends modern-version error, saying the verse has living earthly unsaved people perishing in an ongoing way, supposedly requiring a parallel clause on living people saved in an ongoing way. That has no basis in fact, for the living unsaved are on a path to destruction, but can be saved, as White admits, and as long as this offer exists, they aren't perishing. Only those in hell now are perishing now. Literal Greek often isn't good English, and translators must know this, as those of the KJB did.

context determines the sense, and *gain* doesn't apply here. The KJB expresses the matter in terms of soul security <u>revealed</u> by patience in trials. Context teaches what Mt.10:22 does in saying, *he that endureth to the end shall be saved*, meaning our salvation is proved if our faith endures injurious trials. In Lk.21:19 the KJB *Possess ye your souls* speaks of mastering our troubles, as in 1 Thess.4:4 (same Greek verb) that tells us to possess (master, not gain) our vessel in sanctification and honor. The KJB has the true Lk.21:19 sense, mastering, possessing the control of, our souls to speak in the power of God's salvation in us so as to foil men who would condemn us by using our words against us. The NIV and NASV support works salvation here.

Like modern textual critics, modern translators seem to have trouble even with matters as basic as salvation. Let's see how they do with matters of science that are presented in God's Word.

6. Job 40:15-24: Modern scholars fear dinosaurs in the Bible

Evolutionists say dinosaurs died out millions of years before man existed, so they say the Bible, that began to be written no more than ~4000 years ago, says nothing of dinosaurs. But Job says God made dinosaurs when He made man (Job), refuting their supposed existence millions of years before man. The term *dinosaur* is modern, so it isn't in the Bible, but Job describes dinosaurs in detail otherwise known only in modern days. It says the man Job lived in Uz, close to the land later called Israel, so dinosaurs roamed that region in pre-Israel days, explaining why Job 40:23 links dinosaurs to the Jordan river. As the one Bible book that speaks of dinosaurs, Job is by far the oldest (see Appendix B).

God speaks to Job of dinosaurs:
15. *Behold now behemoth, which <u>I made with thee</u>; he eateth grass.*
16. *...his strength is in his loins, and his force is in the navel of his belly.*
17. *He moveth his tail like a cedar...*

18. *His bones are as strong pieces of brass; his bones are like bars...*
19. *He is the chief of the ways of God...*
21. *He lieth under the shady trees...*
23. *Behold, he drinketh up a river and hasteth not: he trusteth that he can draw up Jordan into his mouth.*
24: *He taketh it with his eyes: his nose pierceth through snares.*

Like Behemoth, a giant titanosaur ate grass. Like behemoth, this dinosaur was *chief of the ways of God*, the largest animal in man's sight on land (as long as 100 ft, as heavy as 100 tons, as tall as a 5-story building & a tail as long as 50 ft.) Only this dinosaur had a tail that moved like a cedar tree in respect of size and force. Behemoth had to be this big to fit figurative language on ingesting a river. In accord with dinosaur facsimilies, strength exertion, like that of behemoth, was centered in the belly to power the huge legs and tail (dinosaurs had no *navel*, but here the term means *center*, the basic dictionary sense). Dinosaurs, unknown to us until the 19th century, fully fit the description of behemoth written in Job ~4000 years ago. Job revealed dinosaurs millennia before man discovered them, so the Bible is the final authority on dinosaurs, and evolutionist speculation cannot compete.

That dinosaurs lived during our history is seen by a find of soft flexible tissue like blood cells in Tyrannosaurus bone fossils said to be 68 million years old; ongoing work refutes evolutionist efforts to disprove soft tissue.[17] This organic matter decays too rapidly in fossilization to last many thousands, let alone millions, of years. Decay is slowed much by burial in flood sediments, but even then, shorter-term decomposition results from unavoidable moisture and natural radioactivity. Sediment from a fairly recent flood would be involved, likely the Great Flood ~4400 years ago.

17. Schweitzer, M.H. et al. *Science.* Vol 307. #5717. p1952-55. Mar. 05. Schweitzer and a large team of scientists confirmed soft tissue in "80 million-yr. old" dinosaur fossil bone. Schweitzer et al. *Paleontology and Archaeology.* April 2009

RSV/NIV/NASV translators don't defy the evolutionist agenda, their footnotes suggesting that behemoth is a hippopotamus. The RSV at 40:17 says *he makes his tail stiff like a cedar*, a linguistic possibility, but "stiff like a twig" would be needed to denote the small hippopotamus tail. In the Hebrew *cedar* is used in the logical/contextual sense of a large tree bending by swaying.

The NASV verse 23 says, *If a river rages, he is not alarmed; he is confident, though the Jordan rushes to his mouth*. The NIV says, *When the river rages, he is not alarmed; he is secure though Jordan should surge against his mouth*. This language masks behemoth's great size and his dinosaur identity, suiting a river-dwelling hippopotamus that's much smaller than a titanosaur; it utilizes wrong syntax and word choice, distorts verse sense and poetic style, and misses verse division into two thoughts.

Passage syntax stresses behemoth's size in reiterative poetic style (behemoth this and behemoth that, *he/his* opening most verses as the subject or subject possessive pronoun, and *he/his/him* signifying behemoth). The style makes *he*, behemoth, the subject of the 4 verse-23 clauses. The NASV/NIV must follow the style and make *he* subjects of very brief 2nd and 3rd clauses, but they deviate to make rivers the subjects of longer 1st and 4th clauses, masking behemoth's size. Verse 23 begins, *Behold* to stress *he*, giant behemoth, as the verse subject. Poetic style and a transitive verb make *river* a direct object in the first clause, and NASV/NIV lack of a direct object for a transitive verb proves poor translation. With *river* as the subject of the first clause and *If /When* replacing *Behold*, the Hebrew sense, in NASV language, is a nonsensical, *If a river rages, he* (a river) *isn't alarmed* and *he* (a river) *is confident, though the Jordan rushes to his* (a river's) *mouth*. To Ignore poetic style and render the incorrect intransitive *rages* makes the subject pronoun *he* linked to this verb in the Hebrew refer to *river* as the clause subject, which relates any subsequent *he/his* in the verse to *river*.

25

He as the subject and the verb as transitive are correct grammar. It's not that a river rages, but that behemoth *drinketh up* a river (poetic language), consuming it in the sense of conquering it,[18] crossing easily, so he *hasteth not* to cross as it's no threat due to his size.[19] This is like the sense of the Job 39:24 *he* (the horse) *swalloweth the ground*, or consumes/conquers terrain[20] (context and poetic-style make *he* a clause subject and *ground* a direct object). Hebrew language requires modern translators to follow this syntax, but they deviate in 40:23 where language makes it possible to imagine *river* as a clause subject. Lamsa's Peshitta shows *river* isn't the subject, saying, *Behold, if he plunges into the river*, but this too avoids the dinosaur identity.[21]

Modern translators must follow poetic style where language ex-cludes alternatives, making behemoth a clause subject in 40:15, 19,21, and other animals clause subjects in 39:3,7,8,14-16,18,21,

18. Jamieson/Fausset/Brown Com. (JFB) accepts the raging-river notion, but has *overwhelm*, reflecting *conquers*, not *rages*. Hebrew-language exp-ert, R. Gordis, says the verb is transitive and calls the raging-river notion, *dubious translation*: Gordis, R. 1978. *The Book of Job. Com., New Trans-lation and Special Studies*. Jewish Theo. Sem. of America. N.Y.C.

19. NIV/NASV *he is not alarmed* isn't justified; the Hebrew verb isn't intransitive stative (state of being with verb *is*), and grammar indicates the KJV intransitive fientive (action) verb *hasteth not* (JFB *trembleth not*).

20. Clarke's Commentary. N.Y. Abingdon-Cokesbury Press.

21. Job 40 Context is one of emphasis as God contrasts His wisdom and power with Job's. The 40:23 first clause and word stress the subject, behe-moth, and include a pause, so *Behold* with a comma or exclamation point is indicated. The RSV/ESV, *Behold, if the river…*is supportive of *Behold* and a pause, but adds *if* to make river a clause subject; it's *Behold* or *If*, not both. *If/when* remove emphasis and the pause. NRSV *Even if the river* …HCSV *though the river…*and NKJV *Indeed the river…*are poor, drop-ping emphasis and a pause. In 40:15, where the 1st clause opens in a way like that of 40:23, modern versions offer *Behold* or an equivalent, with a pause, as they must, for behemoth is named there (NASV, *Behold now Behemoth, …*and NIV, *Look at the behemoth, …*), but they open 40:23 differently; they mask the dinosaur identity and avoid defying evolutionists.

22,24,25. But 40:23 is susceptible to imagining an alternative, as is 40:17. In the NIV, 40:17 is altered the way 40:23 is altered, deviating from poetic style and context to make the tail the subject, and stressing tail motion over size to mask the dinosaur identity even further. Other modern versions don't deviate this way in 40:17, and there was no proper reason to do so in 40:23.

Another thought arises from that above, that behemoth *trusteth that he can draw up Jordan into his mouth*, which has a dual sense. Figuratively, *draw up*, like *drinketh up*, means behemoth conquers Jordan, now in the sense of traversing its length, drawing all the way up into Jordan's (his) mouth (now *his* refers to Jordan, for it's a case of behemoth drawing up into Jordan's mouth, not an absurd rushing of a river to Jordan's mouth). *Draw up* is literally *drink* (poetic exaggeration; a Heb. athnah at *hasteth* stipulates a colon, the second thought developing the first to suggest a size great enough to imagine ingesting of a river).[22]

The NASV/NIV miss the second thought, making the two one, and missing the nature of Jordan's flow. It's not that Jordan *rushes/surges*; poetic style and a transitive verb make *behemoth* the subject and *Jordan* a direct object, and the verb as a transitive means *bring forth*, *draw up* (NKJV *into his mouth* and Brenton's Septuagint *up into his mouth are fine*, but their use of verbs similar to *rushes*/surges distorts verse sense).

In missing the second thought, the NASV/NIV reiterate the first in new words, as typical of Hebrew poetry. But the first isn't just reiterated; it's developed with more meaning to construct a second, as noted above. *He is confident/secure* only justifies *though the Jordan rushes* and the wrong raging-river concept to make Jordan the subject of a clause unrelated to context on behemoth's size. A

---

22. The Hebrew imperfect verb can be rendered fientive *trusteth*, or stative *is confident*. Grammar suggests either is correct, but *trusteth* better reflects verse syntax, context and poetic style (see latter part of above paragraph on p28), and *is confident* serves only to support the raging-river distortion.

KJV *that* in *that he can draw up Jordan* gives proper syntax, tying *trusteth* to a clause with the object of trust, conquest of Jordan, to construct the second thought by more proper emphasis on behemoth's size. Job 40:24 also stresses the size, saying he takes Jordan *with his eyes* (owns it) and destroys snares (traps). A hippo is too small to justify all the figurative size description, so Jordan is made the 4th clause subject.

The NASV/NIV lose both verse-23 thoughts by wrong syntax and word choice, emphasizing rivers twice when behemoth's great size is the one emphasis. Dinosaurs are well known today, but modern translators hide them, perhaps being fearful of defying evolutionists. Dinosaurs were unknown in 1611, yet the KJV is correct, marking a Providentially-ordained version.

Modern translators don't do too well with science, and we'll forget this topic for awhile and see how well they do with history.

7. Unique Hebrew-text history confuses modern translators
In modern versions Elhanen kills Goliath at 2 Samuel 21:19, but David kills him at 1 Samuel 17, all in accord with literal Hebrew. Critics suggest copyist error or a passage contradiction.

2 Samuel 21:19
...Elhanen the son of Jaare-oregim, a Bethlehemite, slew <u>the</u> <u>brother of</u> Goliath the Gittite, the staff of whose spear was like a weaver's beam.

1 Chronicles 20:5
...Elhanen the son of Jair slew Lahmi the brother of Goliath the Gittite, whose spear staff was like a weaver's beam.

At 2 Samuel 21:19 an italicized KJB *the brother of* is correct, as in 1 Chronicles. The 2 Samuel Hebrew text doesn't contradict that of 1 Samuel 17. In 1 and 2 Samuel *Goliath* is a symbolic name for two different giants, and Chronicles specifies Elhanen's giant. The KJB applies this to 2 Samuel to prevent confusion. Early Hebrew readers would know *Goliath* was symbolic, and Chronicles later prevented confusion, but modern scholars are still confused.

Israel wouldn't know proper names of invading strangers, for God required separation from idol-worshippers like the Philistines. 2 Samuel assigns to giants symbolic names signifying great size, except for a verse 21:20 giant denoted by his unique limbs, a clear indication his proper name was unknown to text scribes. All giants in our texts are of one family (or tribe), and in 21:16,18 the head of the family is called *the giant*, indicating his proper name was unknown to text scribes, so names of his sons were unknown. But Hebrew giant-killers in 2 Samuel 21 have proper names and are noted as sons of men with proper names (the scribes would know proper names of their countrymen). The name contrast clearly shows proper names of the giants were unknown. In the much-later Chronicles, Hebrew names don't change, as expected of proper names, but names of certain giants change, invented proper names being assigned, as we'll see.

One suggestion of a Hebrew-name change is *Jaare-oregim* (*forests of weavers*) in Samuel, called *Jair* in Chronicles. *Oregim* (*weavers*), an added symbolic name discarded in Chronicles, attaches to *Jaare* to stress the son's valor in defeating a man so big his spear shaft was like a weaver's beam. Despite a new meaning, *Jair* (*he arouses/rises* [against]), isn't a different name, just a variant of *Jaare* in the later Chronicles. *Jair*, spelled much like *Jaare*, retains the man's identity, and the new meaning still reflects the son's valor to compensate for loss of *oregim*. This is indicated, for *Jair* derives from a margin note (qere), a textual comment serving here to up-date spelling.[23]

23.*Jarre-oregim* is said to be a scribal error joining *oregim* (*weavers*) to *Jaare, weavers beam* being nearby in the text. Error is claimed, as *forests of weavers* isn't a man's name. But *oregim* is a symbolic name tied to a proper one, *Jaare*, resulting in a compound name that can't be translated as one, as *Ed the giant*, isn't *Ed Giant*. And error is claimed since *oregim* isn't in the Chronicles name, but Chronicles discards symbolic names, as we'll see. *Oregim* added to *Jaare* would observe the son's valor. In Hebrew patriarchal society, with men identified by the fathers' names (son of Saul, Jesse, etc.) recognizing a father for his son's deeds is no surprise

Goliath as symbolic of great size is indicated by use of that type of name for a giant killed by Sibbechai (2 Sam.21:18), *Saph*, the name of the head of an Arabic family in Palestine with sons of great height and strength (Jamieson, Fausset, Brown com), so it signifies great size. And a giant killed by Abishai, *Ishbi-benob* (*my seat is on a high place*) signifies one of great stature or size.

A symbolic *Goliath* for Elhanen's giant, and a mutual Bethlehem origin, relate Elhanen to David. David killed the first Goliath as Israel cowered before him, and God raised up Bethlehemites inspired by David's example to handle giants. If another Bethlehemite kills a giant, David's leadership is recognized, indirectly or directly, and *Goliath* and *Bethlehemite* do so indirectly (another Goliath bites the dust; David is great!) David is recognized directly as 2 Sam.21:21 identifies David's brother as the father of Bethlehemite giant-killer, Jonathan. This giant needs no name, his unique physical features identifying him. Such recognition of David's leadership appears in 2 Sam.8:13 regarding his nephew Abishai's victory over Edomite Syrians of 1 Chron.18:12.

David is recognized directly as Abishai is called a son of Zeruiah (David's sister) in 2 Sam.21:17. *Goliath* doesn't apply, as Abishai evidently wasn't a Bethlehemite. He wasn't in Jesse's descent line, his mother Zeruiah being David's sister (1 Chro.2: 15,16) by marriage of David's mother to Jesse after marriage to Nahash (2 Sam.17:25). Nahash is an Ammonite name in 1 Sam. 11:1, and Zeruiah's sister Abigail married an Ishmaelite (1 Chro. 2:17), so the family of Nahash seems not to be basically Israelite. *Goliath* also doesn't apply to the giant of Sibbechai, a Hushathite unrelated to David. *Saph* and *Ishbi-benob* distinguish giants of non-Bethlehemites, not called as giant-killers, but following the Bethlehemite example. David's link to Elhanen established his leadership in this matter, and avoiding other *Goliath* use helped prevent reader confusion, while Chronicles ensured against it.

Chronicles identifies Elhanen's giant as a brother of the Goliath killed by David (giants' family relationships would be known by reputation). Chronicles assigns a few giants proper names based on identities of the Hebrews who killed them, the only basis other than symbolic names Israel had to differentiate giants. In Chronicles the giant *Saph*, killed by Sibbechai, is *Sippai*, and the latter reflects salient parts of <u>Sibbechai</u>, indicating a Hebrew proper name invented for this giant (*Sa* is now *Si*, and the double consonant *pp* reflects *bb* - the Hebrew for *p* and *b* are phonetically related labials pronounced by emphasizing use of the lips, and *ai* is a common Hebrew-name suffix - eg. Abishai Barzillai, Haggai etc). *Lahmi* (*my bread*) is a Hebrew proper name derived from Elhanen's Beth-<u>lehem</u>-ite origin (*lehem* is *bread*).[24] This Hebrew name for Elhanen's giant differentiates giants of David and Elhanen, yet continues association of the two Hebrews by their Bethlehem origin, and also recognizes David's valor.

That *Goliath* was symbolic couldn't be retained indefinitely, so in Chronicles, written ~500 years after Samuel, *Goliath* is made a proper name for David's giant and proper ones are invented for other giants. The KJB follows Chronicles with italics respecting the Hebrew to preserve passage context and meaning.

Modern translators let a famous account seem inaccurate and cause many to view scripture as faulty stories unsuited as a guide in life. Maybe we'd better look at how they handle theology.

<u>24</u>. *my bread* (livelihood) reflects Nu.14:9 calling giants *bread for us*. Now as *Lahmi* is from *Bethlehemite*, it's said the latter is a corruption of *Lahmi, brother of*. But the text shows Hebrew scribes didn't know proper names, inventing *Lahmi* long after Samuel was written. To incur the error *'-t Lahmi* had to be read as *Bét hal-Lahmi*, an error far too great for a meticulous Hebrew scribe. He'd have to mistake the definite direct-object sign (*'-t*) for a word, *b-t*, and a word for *brother* (*'-h*) for the direct-object sign. He won't mistake a grammar-principle term for a word any more than we'll mistake English punctuation marks for words. Scribes steadily reviewed the text, so it isn't credible to attribute to them three major errors in part of one verse, the two noted here and that regarding *oregim*. Thus it's said they misread a smudged or abraded manuscript, but far from being an error, *Bethlehemite* shows why *Goliath* is used for giants of David and Elhanen.

8. **Micah 5:2 Modern-translator theological confusion**
   KJB

But thou, Bethlehem Ephratah, though thou be little among the thousands of Judah, yet out of thee shall he come forth unto me that is to be ruler in Israel; whose goings forth have been from of old, from everlasting.
   RSV
…whose origin is from of old, from ancient days.
   NIV
…whose origins are from of old from ancient times.

This one from Bethlehem whose goings forth (correct Hebrew) are from everlasting is eternal Christ without beginning of days. To say He has an origin suggests He's a mere man of ancient times. The Hebrew for *origin* is plural, and the NIV *origins* suggests reincarnation, evidently a case of translator theological confusion.

9. **Modern scholars miss theology regarding God's Spirit**
Scholars criticize KJV use of both *Holy Ghost* and *Holy Spirit*, as if use of two terms lends credence to Mormon dogma on viewing the Spirit as a person at times and as a force other times. This is great error by scholars and Mormons. The two terms distinguish our heavenly and earthly perspectives of the Spirit. Readers should note that in the 1 Jn.5:7,8 Johannine Comma (so erroneously discredited by scholars), *Holy Ghost* refers to the heavenly third person of the Trinity, and *Spirit* refers to the work of the Holy Ghost in Jesus. He's a person, but our perspective of Him varies with context locale and the manner of His work. He is eternally in the heavenly Trinity, but was also part of the Savior's person on earth, as He is part of a true Christian's person on earth today.

   The dual perspective is seen in 1 Pet.1:12 that says *the Holy Ghost sent down from heaven* (from the heavenly Trinity) and 1 Cor.2:10 that says *But God hath revealed them* (things God prepares for His own) *by his Spirit: for the Spirit searcheth all things*…Thus to receive the Holy Ghost sent from heaven is to receive the form by which He works on earth, the Holy Spirit,

Spirit, Spirit of Christ, Spirit of God and other such terms.

The two perspectives can be contrasted. The KJV Lk.3:22 refers to the Holy Ghost descending on the Savior in the form of a dove. In Mk.1:10 the Spirit descends upon him like a dove, and in Mt.3:16 the Spirit of God descends upon Him like a dove. Luke gives the heavenly perspective, and Mark and Matthew give the earthly, while Matthew suggests the heavenly also.

Another contextual factor applies. When the Holy Ghost is noted in the text as speaking, He speaks of Himself in the first person, while the Spirit speaks without referencing His own person (ie: Acts 13:2 - *the Holy Ghost said, separate* me *Barnabus and Saul* …but in Acts 8:29 – *the Spirit said unto Philip, Go near and join thyself to this chariot*). Intensity of personal reference seems to affect term use, as also seen in Mt.12:31,32 where blasphemy is committed against the Holy Ghost, but in Heb.10:29 someone does *despite unto the Spirit* (insults), and Eph.4:30 says *grieve not the Holy Spirit.* In Acts 5:3 two people lie to the Holy Ghost, but in Acts 5:9 the two tempt the Spirit of the Lord. Often this intensity differentiation isn't sharp, and a differentiation of Jack Moorman (www.alexanderhamiltoninstitute.org) can apply, that *Holy Ghost* signifies the separate person of the Trinity, while Spirit terms signify association with the Father or Christ.

Regardless of the rendering, the Greek is always *pneuma*, and always refers to a person in reference to God in any context. We receive, are filled by, and led by, He who is called the Holy Ghost or various Spirit names, changes being in our perspective, intensity of personal reference or relationship to the Father and Son.

A Look at the Thinking of a Modern Critic of the KJB

We wonder why scholars today have so much trouble representing scripture in theology, doctrine, history and science. We might find out by examining their thinking on text renderings. We do so with the late K. Wuest, Greek professor at Moody Bible Institute.

10. **1 Thes.4:13-18: The Rapture.** Wuest sees much meaning in Greek *harpazo* that he says isn't in the KJB *caught up*. He says *harpazo* signifies "carried off by force," the Rapture being forceful to defeat satan and demons trying to keep saints from heaven. He sees a second sense, "claiming for oneself eagerly," for Christ is a bridegroom. He sees a third sense, "to rescue from destruction," which he feels means saving the church from Tribulation destruction. He sees a fourth sense, "to snatch away," saying the Rapture will be sudden, catching Satan and everyone by surprise.

Any of these can apply to the Rapture, but all can't apply in one context. In translation a term meaning to best fit context is chosen. None of the noted meanings is justified by context, let alone one word in the context, and a general *caught up* is proper. "Carried off by force" can apply to the Rapture, but to say it's to defeat Satan's effort to keep saints from heaven is imagination not justified by the Greek word, context or scripture as a whole. And in the Rapture, Christ takes His bride to Himself, but that's noted elsewhere (Rev.21:1-9). Further, scripture indicates Pre-Tribulation Rapture, but to say this is to rescue from danger is to suppose facing danger before rescue, which can't be deduced from this word and context. And the Rapture will be sudden, but this is revealed elsewhere (1 Cor.15:52) and isn't done to surprise the devil. Wuest sees many meanings in one word, but they derive from imagination and word nuances in various contexts.

11. Wuest distinguishes the 1 Thess.4:17 *air* (Gr.*aer*), the lower atmosphere, from the upper stratosphere (Gr. *aither*), saying non-Greek readers might envision the stratosphere. But *aither*, of Greek mythology, isn't in the New Testament, so the distinction is irrelevant to biblical Greek. Yet passage context saying saints will *meet the Lord in the air*, also says they'll be *caught up...in the clouds*, and clouds in the stratosphere are rare and thin. The Greek text doesn't make distinctions of modern science, yet English readers get this from our 17th century KJB preceding the modern-science era, a mark of Providential guidance.

Authenticity: God as the Ultimate Author of the True Text

We've looked at what modern scholars do to the text, and it looks like we've got to look earnestly for what God does to the text.

God's text-dictation accounts for inerrancy of the true text

Plenary/verbal inspiration requires dictation of each word to writer minds by the Spirit to achieve inerrancy. Scholars dismiss dictation due to human input in the form of writing style and supposed error in scripture. Consistent KJB accuracy defies the notion of error, and human writing style is seen since, contrary to how scholars define it, dictation doesn't suspend writer intellect.

1. Verbatim dictation eliminates writing style, as in Exod.34:27 that says, *And the Lord said unto Moses, Write thou these words* ...Jer.30:2 says *Thus speaketh the Lord God of Israel, saying, Write thee all the words that I have spoken to thee in a book.*

A vision dictates to a writer's eye and ear. Rev.1:10,11 says *...I was in the Spirit on the Lord's day, and heard behind me a great voice, as of a trumpet, saying...What thou seeest, write in a book...*In dictation to the ear in Rev.2:1, Christ in the vision says *Unto the angel of the church of Ephesus write; These things saith he...*Intact faculties are indicated, for in 1:10 John hears a voice behind him and turns and gives details of what he sees. In 1:17 he falls at the feet of Christ in the vision, as expected of one with intact faculties confronted by a representation of God.

Dr. Phil Stringer, Ravenswood Baptist Church, Chicago, notes God spoke to Balaam by his donkey. Num.22:28 says, *And the Lord opened the mouth of the ass, and she said unto Balaam, What have I done unto thee, that thou hast smitten me these three times?* The ass, devoid of any speaking style, spoke her feelings to Balaam. She seems intellectually involved, an impossibility, so God preserved her "viewpoint." Thus preserved viewpoints, and thus mental faculties, of scripture penmen is expected.

2. In dictation a writer can show usual intellect and style as Holy Ghost control of his writing by-passes his awareness. Consider

Jesus' mother Mary *great with child* (Lk.2:5) in Nazareth ~75 miles from Bethlehem. If she knew the Mic.5:2 prophecy on a Bethlehem birth, in the hardship of the final stage of pregnancy, she'd dread a donkey ride to Bethlehem. And Joseph would dread hazards of labor pains, premature delivery or miscarriage in a lonely area on the way. God had to handle these details, but how would He get her to Bethlehem? He'd stir-up the mind of the pagan Caesar Augustus, to see a need to finance the empire in better ways than resented harsh taxes (Lk.2:1-5). There likely was fear of tax rebellion then (Acts 5:37 notes tax rebellion when the Roman governor of Syria was Cyrenius, who ruled earlier as Mary and Joseph went to Bethlehem-Lk.2:2).[25] God would move Caesar to require empire residents to enroll for taxation at their native cities so local authorities could verify ties to family assets (an old private-contractor system could use locals to be fair, but publicans like Zaccheus would cheat). All would pay by ability, the masses not being affected enough to incite rebellion (that occurred later). Augustus began a graduated income/property tax (Thompson says Augustus began the tax enrollment, as is logical since it accords with his *Pax Romana*, a time of relative peace, prosperity and tax reform).[26] The tax summons was timed too close to the Child's birth for delivery before Mary and Joseph had to go to Bethlehem, so they came in timely fashion to their city of origin as descendants of David. Thus God subtly dictated acts of many people in a vast empire without anyone knowing it.

3. Regarding word dictation, in Ps.22:8 David speaks words of persecutors who taunt him, saying *He trusted on the Lord that he would deliver him: let him deliver him...*This prophesies words spoken by Jesus' persecutors at the Cross 1000 years later. In Mt.27:43, priests, elders and scribes taunt Jesus saying, *He trusted in God; let him deliver him*. The prophecy is fulfilled on behalf of Jesus by His worst enemies, authenticating Him as the

25. *King James Bible Commentary*. 1999. Nashville. Nelson. p1343.
26. Thompson, J.A. 1962. *The Bible and Archaeology*. Eerdmans. p375.

Son of David, God's Messiah, the last thing in the world they would willingly do. Had they known this meaning, they would never have spoken these words. Thus dictation by-passes speaker awareness, and makes use of malicious free-will word choice and speaking style and literal word meaning. It's said they mocked Jesus with David's prophecy, but they revered David and would not identify themselves with men vilifying him. And they would never relate prophetic words of David to Jesus, lest they present prophecy authenticating Jesus as the Messiah. Actually they'd not see the verse as prophecy useful in feigned fulfillment, for, of itself, it's indicative only of David's history, not of prophecy.

Now did the Spirit work in men just used by satan? In Mt.27: 42 they opposed salvation, saying of Jesus, *let him now come down from the Cross, and we will believe him*. The alternative is God putting just the right men with just the right free-will mindset in just the right place to fulfill His will in just the right way. With the prophecy made ~1000 years before the Cross, this would mean God logistically or genetically controlled people in ~40-50 generations for 1000 years, intervening in free-will decisions to invoke His will. Mt.10:29,30 supports this, saying, *Are not two sparrows sold for a farthing? And one of them shall not fall on the ground without your Father. But the very hairs of your head are all numbered.*

If the Spirit did not speak through these men, dictation was indirect, by control of many generations. Otherwise it was direct, using minds and speaking styles of evil men against their will.

Thus the Spirit can dictate to His servants, unknown to them (thought motivation). Lk.1:3 says, *It seemed good to me also, having had perfect understanding of all things from the very first, to write*...Luke seems to write at a whim by memory, but the Spirit directing without his awareness explains, *It seemed good ...to write,* which explains his *perfect* understanding...Now we see the verse very differently. Luke writes in his style and intellect, and the Spirit motivates his free will, supervising by allowing or disallowing word choice (i.e. keep this word Luke, not that one). God dictates each word, editing words produced by Luke's intellect and style to avoid all appearance of dictation. 2 Pet.1: 20,21 suggests such inspiration, saying *the prophecy came not in old time by the will of man: but holy men of God spake as they were moved by the Holy Ghost* (words willed by the Spirit).

4. In Ps.69 David tells of his persecution in words linked to those of the Son of David on the Cross 1000 years later. David's words begin a dual reference to himself and Jesus in vss.7-20. In vs.21, he speaks only Jesus' words of His persecution and toxic gall and pain-killing vinegar offered to Him (Mt.27:34), and such words continue to vs.36. Transition from David's words to those of Jesus is like parting a curtain to reveal Christ dictating all words from the start. David speaks humanly of himself, but his words that are Jesus' words refer only figuratively to himself and are those he wouldn't normally say of himself, indicating dictation.

5. A 3-fold dictation in Zech.11:12,13, prophecy on betrayal of Jesus for 30 pieces of silver, says, *So they weighed for my price thirty pieces of silver. And the LORD said unto me, Cast it unto the potter...And I took the thirty pieces of silver, and cast them to the potter in the house of the Lord.* The speaker of *my price* can only be Christ pre-incarnate speaking by (dictating to) Zechariah. Covetous Judas, after the betrayal, is moved in his mind (dictated to) by Christ to do the right thing, return the blood money to elders and priests; he casts it down in the temple in disgust at what he's done, selling his soul for money. And cruel covetous priests and elders causing the Crucifixion used the money for the potter's field to bury strangers (Gentiles they normally didn't care about), being moved in their minds (dictated to) by Christ to use the money rightly. Christ figuratively cast the silver to the potter, in the house of the Lord, by dictating thoughts of Judas, priests and elders.

6. Jonah 2 In recent history, scientists classified *fish* as water dwellers with gills, fins and skeletons of bone or cartilage. But earlier the term included all creatures living habitually in water, including lung-breathing whales. The early meaning persists in language convention of scientists themselves, such as *jellyfish* and *starfish*, terms they apply to creatures with no skeleton or fins and *lungfish* that they apply to one with gills and lungs. Thus the term in Jonah is the early one with a more inclusive meaning, and the KJB Mt.12:40 *whale* is the specific large water-dweller.

Jonah's whale: It's said a man swallowed by a big fish has no air and can only be a meal. Some say Jonah died and was resurrected. But the KJV says, *When my soul fainted within me, I remembered the Lord*, so his soul nearly parted, but didn't (other versions are similar here). Some call the account symbolic, but Christ calls it literal, equating Jonah's 3-day hell-like trip in the whale with His soul's 3-day sojourn in hell where He descended after the Cross to conquer this enemy (Mt.12:40).

The Greek for the KJV Mt.12:40 *whale* has various meanings, the right one being determined by context. Scientific context study shows *whale* is the basis for Jonah's 3-day survival in the fish, and that the account is literal realty not requiring miracles. Context reveals the fish as a whale in saying it dives to great depths in the sea. Jonah's fish takes him to the bottoms of mountains (and so the sea), and there are submerged mountain ranges in the Mediterranean, west of the seaport Jonah sailed from. Whales are the only large sea creatures that dive to great depths in the sea. Sperm whales often exceed the average depth of the Mediterranean, ~5000 ft, and have reached nearly 10,000 ft. A sperm whale is the one whale that dives to such depths and is big enough to swallow a man. It has swallowed giant squid and sharks larger than a man.

Regarding ingestion of Jonah by a sperm whale, the creature's teeth are limited to the lower jaw, and are for seizing prey. It swallows prey and "chews" by crushing contraction in the first of its multiple stomachs. It eats squid or fish, and a clothing-covered Jonah would offer an alien taste that wouldn't induce contraction. The first stomach doesn't produce digestive juices, and an opening to the second is too small to admit Jonah for chemical digestion. He would give the whale a stomach ache, which is why he was later vomited up (at God's command). To protect Jonah from crushing contraction in the first stomach, the whale had to fast three days, and it often fasts when food is scarce, living off its own blubber.

When under extreme pressure at great depth in the sea, the body of a sperm whale resists crushing, and stomach functions are maintained since the whale swallows giant squid while at depth. The whale is protected from filling of its multiple stomachs with seawater under extreme pressure when eating since that not only would prevent chemical digestion in the second stomach, but would destroy the digestive system and kill the whale. Evidently, before the whale opens its mouth to swallow prey, the esophagus closes off the stomachs to water entry, and after the mouth closes, the esophagus opens to admit the prey. Limited seawater entering the stomach with the prey would be the source of limited seawater normally present in the first stomach to supply whale body fluid needs. The stomach must be immune to effects of extreme pressure under all conditions, and clearly so when the whale wasn't eating. With Jonah in its stomach, it wouldn't eat due to the stomach ache, and Jonah would be fully protected from extreme pressure.

Under pressure, nitrogen from air dissolves in blood, and bubbles out in the circulatory system in rapid ascents, threatening death (bends sickness). A sperm whale ascends rapidly, but in charging its blood and muscles with oxygen from the air for a dive, the nitrogen taken in is mostly absorbed in foam in sinuses for later discharge in the spout. This effect and collapse of the lungs in a dive greatly limit nitrogen access to a whale's blood stream. Non-availability of this nitrogen source to the stomach, and minimal internal pressure there, would protect Jonah from the bends.

Jonah's most crucial need was air to breathe. The whale breathes through a top-side blowhole, but it forces air into is stomachs in breaching head-first out of the water, as it might do in swallowing Jonah (nitrogen in air should be absorbed by whale oil). This could not give Jonah enough oxygen to survive a deep dive, so normal isolation of respiratory-system air from the stomachs had to be bridged somehow, as Jonah 1:17 indicates, saying God *prepared* the fish (not the NIV/NASV *provided* or *appointed* that don't address the needed irregularity in whale anatomy. Oxygen stored in whale blood hemoglobin and muscles during preparation for a dive had to be tapped. Preparation might involve a birth defect admitting blood oxygen into the digestive tract when the whale wasn't eating (that would indicate God knew all about the Jonah incident long before it occurred). Or preparation might involve bleeding of the first stomach due to contraction in the presence of sharp debris found at times in whale stomachs. Carbon dioxide (CO_2) increases in whale blood as oxygen is consumed in a dive, releasing oxygen from whale hemoglobin for Jonah. In the process oxygen in muscles might be tapped. CO_2 is released later, and build-up of this and that in Jonah's breath could suffocate him, mandating brief time at depth and new air. When the whale is at depth, oxygen mainly supplies its brain, little being needed by muscles, and Jonah's use would deprive the brain to induce early ascent for air. And a sick whale, though habitually diving for food, wouldn't eat, or stay long at depth, as necessary to protect Jonah. He nearly died, but would recover as the whale swam to land, forcing in new air in periodic breaching due to the stomach ache. If oxygen reached the stomach due to a birth defect, all whale surface breathing would steadily supply oxygen to Jonah.

Jonah, written ~2800 years ago, agrees with modern knowledge of whale technology. How can this be when the ancient writer couldn't know matters like the unique whale digestion processes, prolonged fasting ability, isolation of a whale respiratory system from the stomach, a need to prepare the whale for Jonah's survival and whale deep diving ability known only in later centuries, especially extreme-depth diving on the order of 5000 feet known to men only by the 20th century with invention of sonar. Jonah, the likely writer, wasn't even a whaler by trade. And how could Jonah inside the whale know he was on the bottom of the sea, at a location near undersea mountains? There is one who knew whale technology 2800 years ago, and knew exact details of Jonah's plight. God is the one who put Jonah through his experience, so He is the author of words describing Jonah's experience. It's as if God put His signature on this Bible book, imparting words to the human writer, Jonah or his associate. A vital related factor revealing God's signature is identification of Jonah's fish as a whale in Mt.12:40, but modern translators don't identify the fish as a whale, in effect, erasing God's signature from the text.

7. John 1:1,3
1. In the beginning was the word...and the word was God
3. All things were made by him...

John couldn't know by his own intellect that Christ is the Word of creation, the speaker of *Let there be*, for nothing in Genesis reveals this. The writing had to be dictated by the Spirit.

8. 2 Cor.4:4-6
For God, who commanded the light to shine out of darkness (Gen.1:3), hath shined in our hearts, to give the light of the knowledge of the glory of God in the face of Jesus Christ.

Only by dictation can Paul relate the Gen.1:3 light of creation to God's glory in Christ's face to reveal Christ's glory as the first sun. Only by dictation can John call Christ the Morning Star (Rev.22:16), the creation-morning light of the world (Jn.8:12).

9. 1 Cor.10:4.
And did all drink the same spiritual drink: for they drank of that spiritual Rock that followed them: and that Rock was Christ.

Paul calls Christ the spiritual rock following Israel (in the wilderness wandering under Moses). Only by dictation can Paul say this, for nothing in the Old Testament relates Christ to the rock.

Authenticity Deduced Textually and Historically

Now we consider how God's hand on the text in inspiration by dictation affects text inerrancy in passages scorned by scholars.

1 John 5:7,8: Textual Evidence of Inerrancy

Scholars disdain the Johannine Comma in 1 Jn.5, due to minor Greek manuscript support, but textual proof of its authenticity is so extensive and intricate that it illustrates inerrancy preservation.

KJV

5:5. *Who is he that overcometh the world, but he that believeth that Jesus is the Son of God?*

5:6. *This is he that came by water and blood, even Jesus Christ; not by water only, but by water and blood. And it is the Spirit that beareth witness, because the Spirit is truth.* (the Comma is the text in bold script below)

5:7. *For there are three that bear record* **in heaven, the Father, the Word, and the Holy Ghost and these three are one.**

5:8. **And there are three that bear witness in earth**, *the Spirit, and the water and the blood: and these three agree in one.*

5:9...*this is the witness of God which he hath testified of his Son.*

NIV

5:6. *This is the one who came by water and blood – Jesus Christ. He did not come by water only, but by water and blood. And it is the Spirit who testifies, because the Spirit is the truth.*

5:7. *For there are three that testify:* ___?___ ___?___ ___?___

5:8. *the Spirit, the water and the blood; and the three are in agreement.*

NASV

5:6. *This is the one who came by water and blood, Jesus Christ; not with water only, but with the water and with the blood.*

5:7. *And it is the Spirit who bears witness, because the Spirit is truth.*

5:8. *For there are three that bear witness, the Spirit and the water and the blood; and the three are in agreement.*

Background

The Comma is in just ten 10th-18th century Greek manuscripts, in the margins of some.[27] It's said Erasmus adopted it due to a falsified Greek manuscript, which is just speculation.[28] Latin texts notably support the Comma, the oldest extant being 5th-8th century Old Latin manuscripts and 3rd–4th century notes.[29,30,31] Priscillian quoted it ~385 A.D, Cyprian ~250 A.D. said *the Father, the Son and the Holy Spirit, and these three are one* (*Word* is *Son*), and Tertullian in 215 A.D. said of the Father, Son and Comforter, *which three are one essence*,[32] a Comma reference.[33]

The earliest known Latin text is a mid-2nd century Old-Latin Italic.[34] Allix, 17th-century, said the Waldensen Bible was *the ancient version called the Italic*,[35] and Kenyon said its New Testament had a Traditional-Text basis (Received-Text ancestor).[36] Tepl/Romaunt Waldensen and Vulgate New Testaments all reflect the Italic, but the two refute the Vulgate at places,[37] likely at Jerome's 4th-century variance from the Traditional Text. Italic history ties the Received Text, and potentially the Comma, to the 2nd century. Actually the Comma proves to be authentic, tying it to the 1st-century autograph, to the Italic of the 2nd century and medieval era, to the Received Text, to the KJV.

Censorship marks Comma history, even in the Latin west. A prologue of Jerome's Vulgate notes its removal in 4th-century manuscripts of his day.[38] In a 5th century council of Carthage, 400 North African bishops affirmed it, despite an anti-Comma Arian threat,[32] so it was a holy standard under attack at that time. Facundus, 6th-century Latin, censored it, claiming that Cyprian quoted the 1 Jn.5:8 *three agree in one*.[29]

Grammatical authentication

A. Comma absence makes a clause improperly divide between verses 7 and 8 to make *the Spirit, the water and the blood* a clause fragment in 5:8 and make a fragment serve as verse 5:7.[39] This syntax error is evidently addressed by unique, but incorrect, NIV punctuation.[40] The NASV masks the problem by clause/verse shuffling that joins the 5:7 fragment to 5:8 and creates a verse 5:7 from the latter half of 5:6. Now early Greek manuscripts had no punctuation or verse nos., but this was resolved in a standard system of Stephanus in the 16th century. Modern translators can't rightly change this language convention in the Johannine Comma passage, while adhering to that convention elsewhere.

B. Comma absence causes a verse 5:7 grammatical-<u>masculine</u> participle, to link directly to the 5:8 grammatical-<u>neuter</u> *Spirit*, *water* and *blood*.[41] New-Testament multiple nouns lack gender agreement, and various gender links occur, but scholars are not comfortable with this masculine-neuter link, and try to resolve the issue.[42] It was rejected by Nolan in the early 19th century and Dr. Hills, Dr. Holland and Dr. Strouse [27,29,43] in recent years, but they didn't refute the link with detailed textual proof. We'll offer detailed textual proof that shows they were correct.

To begin with, we note the three neuters aren't encumbered by immediate links to other nouns and can act in unison as one neuter, so linking them to one masculine participle clearly would be contrary to Greek grammar. As we'll see, the 1 Jn.5:7 masculine participle doesn't directly link to the three neuters, yet a verse 5:8 masculine participle in the Comma does just that since the neuters act in unison, in a unique way. This becomes clear as we study two aspects of grammar involving the Comma, and relate our conclusions to context.

1. In verse 5:7 the Comma *Father*, *Word* and *Holy Ghost* is the subject of the participle that is an adjectival substantive (noun-like term) functioning as an appositive that denotes and describes its subject, repeating grammatical gender when possible, and the participle repeats that of the Comma masculine *Father* and *Word*.

Now some will object, saying the participle is the subject, for it appears first in 5:7, in accord with a perceived grammar rule. But that's an over-generalization of the rule. Word order can't consistently determine the subject/appositive relationship, for it varies among passages according to emphasis. A term is commonly emphasized in the Greek by bringing it forward in a clause or a sentence. In verse 5:7 emphasis on *three*, a triune witness that follows and expands a singular 5:6 Spirit witness, places *three* before the divine names to make the participle appear first. The participle is an adjectival substantive that denotes divine persons and describes their role, as expected in its appositive role. The participle fills the adjectival appositive role, and Trinity names, nominatives, are the subject, so rule over-generalization causes a mere apparent subject/appositive reversal. Emphasis on the real subject would rearrange language, as noted below.

"For the Father, the Word and the Holy Ghost (subject), that bear record (appositive) in heaven, are three, and these three are one. And the Spirit, the water and the blood (subject), that bear witness (appositive) on earth, are three, and the three agree in one.

Another subject/appositive apparent reversal by emphasis is in Jn.14:26 that says in the Greek, *But the Comforter, the Holy Ghost,…Comforter* is noted first, for Jesus emphasizes a need of comfort to His disciples. *Holy Ghost* is the subject, and the term *Comforter* is the appositive, an adjectival noun that denotes the Holy Ghost and describes His role.

1 Jn.5:6 illustrates an adjectival participle as an appositive, with emphasis on the Spirit clearly revealing Him as the subject. Here we read, *And it is the Spirit* (subject) *that beareth witness* (the appositive), *because the Spirit is truth.*

2. The verse 5:7 masculine participle links to the Trinity in the Comma for another reason, one that eliminates all multiple-noun grammatical-gender issues. Predicate-nominative grammar *three are one* treats *Father*, *Son* and *Holy Ghost* as a <u>single natural-masculine essence</u>, so the 5:7 participle is grammatically masculine, grammatical and natural gender often corresponding, yet participle plurality treats Trinity persons as individuals. Grammar in verse 7, including the Comma portion, describes the unique 3-in-1 nature of the Trinity, and the Comma portion in this verse is authenticated by the participle outside the Comma.

Now the verse-7 description of the Trinity 3-in-one nature was known only to God when 1 John was written, so John didn't write this on the basis of his own knowledge, indicating the Comma portion in verse 5:7, like the rest of the verse, is inspired by the Spirit.* The deity of Jesus Christ and the Spirit were known early, but the relationship of Trinity persons in verse 7, including the Comma portion, was unknown to men in the latter 1st century when 1 John was written. Elsewhere in scripture the Trinity is only implied, so discrediting the Comma effectively removes the one direct scriptural testimony to the Trinity doctrine.

The Trinitarian pattern repeats as verse 5:8 *three agree in one* (oneness) treats grammatical-neuter *Spirit*, *water* and *blood* as one natural-masculine essence of deity in Jesus, resulting in a 5:8 grammatical-masculine participle in the Comma, grammatical and natural masculinity corresponding; yet participle plurality reveals individuality of three neuters of one essence, reflecting the image of the Trinity in Jesus Christ (we'll soon verify this).

---

*This description of the nature of the Trinity did not emerge until the writings of Tertullian in the early 3rd century. And uniqueness of the Trinity and its tie to the neuters would make Comma validity seem uncertain in the early church, delaying quoting of it. It was cautiously referenced by Tertullian in the early 3rd century. Cyprian quoted it essentially, but cautiously, in the mid-3rd century, his *Son* in place of *Word* avoiding a direct tie to 1 Jn.5:7. It was fully recognized by the late 4th century when even the non-Trinitarian Priscillian quoted it fully.

Contextual authentication of the Comma

Affirmative context: 5:7 masculines *three* and the participle *that bear record* refer to *Father*, *Word* and *Holy Ghost*, the participle reflecting natural masculinity of the three of the Trinity (as well as grammatical masculinity of *Father/Word*), and a 5:8 identical number and participle refer to *Spirit*, *water* and *blood*. As *Father*, *Word* and *Holy Ghost* in heaven testify of Jesus, so *Spirit*, *water* and *blood* in Jesus on earth testify of Him. Parallelism ties natural-masculine *Father, Word* and *Holy Ghost* to grammatical-neuter nouns to relate natural-masculine <u>sense</u> to the neuters, justifying indication of a masculine participle by a relation of *three agree in one* to the Trinity *three are one*. The Trinity illuminates the neuters, and they reflect the image of the Trinity in the Savior.[44]

And with the Comma present, verse 5:9 sums-up 5:7,8, saying, *this is the witness of God* (5:7 Comma-Trinity witness) *which he hath testified of His Son* (5:8 Comma earthly witness in Jesus). And Comma Trinity witness of Jesus reflects John's gospel and other epistles; in Jn.5:37; 8:18; 1:1,14; 16:13,14; 1 Jn.5:6 the *Father*, the *Word* and *Spirit* testify of Jesus.* And *Spirit, water/blood* (of Jesus) testify on earth, verifying the Comma, *And there are three that bear witness <u>in</u> earth*. And Comma absence omits *Word*, John's name for Christ (Jn.1:1, 1 Jn.1:1,14, Rev.19: 13). And *three agree in one*, referring to three divine aspects of Jesus' person, implies comparison with *three are one* of the Comma Trinity.

Conclusive context: Above-noted grammatical/contextual points fit into proof of Comma authenticity that emerges as we study the main topic of 1 John in chapters 4 and 5. John declares Jesus is God incarnate to refute Gnostic-type attacks on His deity. 1 Jn.4: 3 denies a docetist claim that Jesus was a spirit that only seemed to have a body, and 1 Jn.5:6-8 denies a cerinthian claim that Jesus

*Language in the Comma is common in scripture penned by John, the term *bear witness* appearing 20 times and a related *bear record*, 8 times.

was a man temporarily indwelled by Christ in a temporary deity. Authenticity proof relates to the verse 5:6 *by water and blood* that scholars say means He came <u>by</u> baptism and blood-shedding, but He came <u>for</u> those acts. 1 Jn.5:5 declares His deity as God's Son as the basis of salvation, and 5:6 further says of His deity, it's *not by water only, but by water and blood (This* relates 5:5 to 5:6, and *For* relates both to 5:7 and the Comma). Greek grammar indicates *by* has the sense, *by means of,*[45] so He came by power of deity signified by water and blood. Now we discuss the signification.

Spirit signifies Jesus' deity by the Holy Spirit. In Rom.8:9 *Spirit of Christ* is equated with *Spirit of God.* In Jn.3:34 the Spirit is in Him beyond measure, joined to His human spirit.

Water signifies Jesus' deity by the word. Washing of water by the word sanctifies (Eph.5:26). Like water, His word cleanses (Jn.15:3). Salvation is by water and the Spirit (Jn.3:5), the Spirit in the word (*living water*, Jn.4:10). *Water* signifies the word of Jesus' human soul, that calmed a storm at sea, tied to the divine Word of heaven, that spoke the universe into existence, both being part of His person.

Blood signifies Jesus' divine nature by the Father. His Acts 20:28 blood is that of God – what but blood of divine nature, free of sin-stain, could remove sin? Human blood forms in a fetus, both parents contributing, and Mary alone can't produce human blood.* In creating Jesus' body from Mary's genetics, the Holy Ghost would exclude her contribution to the blood to eliminate any sin-stain (the *precious blood of Christ* -1 Pet.1:19). The Holy Ghost would impart to the blood the deity of the Father, who is thus revealed as part of Jesus' person. Jesus said *the Father is in me*, Jn.10: 38, and the blood is the logical way this would apply.

*Human blood forms in the fetus, both parents contributing, but with just one human parent, human blood cannot form (*20 Tremendous Truths*. Baptist Bible tribune. Springfield, MO

Col.2:9 says, *in Him dwelleth all the fullness of the Godhead bodily,* the Holy Ghost by the Spirit, Christ by the Word and the Father by the blood. The body was human, joined to His human soul and spirit, the body being created from the genetics of Mary, a descendant of David. Rom.1:3 says...*Jesus Christ, our Lord, which was made of the seed of David according to the flesh.*

He came by divine power of *Spirit*, *water* and *blood,* elements of His person that signify the divine Trinity (Son of God, Christ) accompanying a human trinity (Son of man, Jesus), deity and humanity being in each part of His person. The divine elements testify of His salvation power as perfect God and perfect man, and so perfect mediator between God and man.

This brings us to how *Spirit, water* and *blood* reflect the natural-masculine Trinity. Each appears in the form of natural-neuter gender of a part (it) of Jesus' person, yet each signifies natural-masculine gender of deity (He) in Jesus by the Comma heavenly Trinity witness. The divine Father testifies of His divine-blood tie to Jesus, so blood (it) <u>signifying</u> the Father reflects masculinity of deity; earthly father/son ties are of blood, and Jesus' divine blood <u>represents</u> the Father/Son tie, finalized by a divine eternal resurrected body with hand and foot wounds (Lk.24:39,40). The divine Word testifies by the water of Jesus' word that He came as the Son in a holy body, so water (it) signifying Him reflects masculinity of deity. The divine Holy Ghost testifies of His earthly role as Jesus' Spirit (it) verifying the water and blood witnesses, so the Spirit on earth reflects masculinity of deity. He came as divine Savior by the power of divine blood (Father) and divine water (Word) attested by the divine Spirit (Holy Ghost). His three aspects of deity *agree in one* essence, reflecting three divine Trinity persons who *are one* essence. Three neuters in Him are treated as the image of the masculine Trinity, requiring a grammatical-masculine participle in verse 5:8 of the Comma, and the participle plurality signifies individuality of the neuters, as in the

Trinity. Since no man knew the basic nature of the Trinity until the early 3rd century, no man could know the exact nature of the image of the Trinity in Jesus Christ any earlier, and the Comma in verse 5:8, like the rest of the verse, is inspired by the Spirit.

Authenticity proved: God's Son came to us, not by water only, or not as the eternal Word (Christ) unembodied, as in docetism, or in some man's body, as in cerinthianism. He came by blood also, <u>divine blood</u> of His own body <u>able</u> to redeem. The body is His, as proved by the divine-blood witness in particular, and by divine Word and Spirit witnesses. As our study shows, the irrefutable witness of the Comma <u>heavenly</u> divine Trinity proves the <u>deity</u> of the Comma <u>earthly</u> *Spirit*, *water* and *blood* witness in Jesus, defeating heresy. Authenticity of the Comma is proved, its heavenly witness and earthly aspect of the *Spirit*, *water* and *blood* witness being vital to 1 Jn.5:6-9 meaning. 1 Jn.5:6-9 is all about truth that refutes gnostic-type heresy attacking Jesus' deity, and the Comma is this truth, its Trinity heavenly witness irrefutably verifying the deity of the earthly witnesses in Jesus Christ.

Likely Comma history

Modern scholars believe Westcott and Hort who said there is no evidence of falsification for dogmatic purposes in any Greek man-uscripts.[46] But Alexandrian texts promoted by these two show evidence of tampering that favors dogma of Gnostics who attacked the deity of Jesus Christ and served the cause of satan who hates Christ and the Trinity, wanting to take the place of the Son of God. In Isa.14:12-15 satan says, *I will be <u>like the most High</u>*, a title reserved for the Son of God). In the Comma the entire Trinity declares the deity of Jesus Christ, so it would be a prime target of Gnostics· It would be deleted in Alexandrian-type Greek texts of "churches" supporting Gnosticism, and many unbiblical churches using the Traditional Text wouldn't safeguard it against this.

The Traditional Text is far superior to the Alexandrian, yet lacks

51

the Comma in most extant manuscripts, and has other differences from the Received Text. This is likely due in part to more limited tampering outside the sphere of Alexandrian influence among the unbiblical churches that handled the Traditional Text. Excellent accuracy and the Comma presence in some manuscripts would be due to periodic text renewal by biblical churches applying an inerrant text preserved from the autographs.

Preservation by renewal is God's plan, marking the beginning of text history as God restored law tables broken by Moses (Ex.32: 15, 34:1). Indeed a Comma presence in 10 later Greek manuscripts, in the text or margins, suggests recognition of a need for renewal and initiation of it. The logical way a renewal would begin is by first placing it in the margin, and the Comma presence in the margins and in the text is evidently preserved to illustrate the beginning and the end of the process for the benefit of readers.

The Traditional Text shows other evidence of renewal in progress. In Eph.3:9 the Received text has the term *fellowship* and a clause, *God who created all things by Jesus Christ.* Alexandrian texts substitute a faulty *administration* for *fellowship* and eliminate *by Jesus Christ* in the verse,[47] elimination of the latter suiting Cerinthians, and *administration* being preferred by Gnostics in general who saw themselves as administrators of hidden knowledge. A Traditional-Text manuscript *by Jesus Christ* is intact, but faulty *adminstration* appears, producing what looks very much like a partially complete renewal frozen in time for centuries, to ensure that readers can see an example of renewal in progress.

The Received Text would finalize a history of text renewals in passages lacking major or earliest Greek support in Traditional-Text history. Any renewal like the Comma in the Received Text, that nullifies Cerinthian dogma depicting Jesus as a mere man, would be of particular note. Notable examples of this are Col.1: 14 on Jesus' blood as crucial to remission of sin and Acts 8:37

on the Ethiopian eunuch who confessed Jesus Christ as the Son of God. The Received Text, as finalized by the KJV translators,[48] corrected limited Traditional-Text error to renew inerrancy for all new true churches established by the printed text.[49]

The Received Text in its final state in the 16th-17th centuries, perfected by outstanding scholars like Erasmus, Stephanus, Beza and KJV translators [48] shows much evidence of being God's final plan for New-Testament text history. Indeed this text and its Johannine Comma declare God's text-renewal plan, following soon after invention of movable-type printing that ended manuscript-tampering potential, and soon after Constantinople in the eastern Roman empire fell and sent Greek scholars west with Traditional-Text manuscripts that were the basis of the Received Text. Soon the Reformation spread this text throughout Europe and later to all churches faithful to the KJV, and soon the text was supplied with chapters, verse numbers and punctuation to greatly enhance readability by all interested parties. Ultimately, the Received Text was the true mark of the end of the Dark Ages in Europe by the light of God's inerrant Word, allowing all to know the true Word for themselves in order to apply it and thus be able to give a proper account of themselves to God one day.

Providential timing in great historical events marks the Received Text, the Comma and all renewals as God's Word preserved from the autographs. And comma potential ties to its autograph by references dating to the early 3rd century and Latin texts dating to the mid-2nd century are now clearly definite ties to the autograph.

Comma authenticity summarized
Comma divine authority refutes two well-known 1st-2nd century heresies. Doceticism was officially denounced in 110 A.D. by Ignatius of Antioch, and Cerinthianism in 170 A.D. by Irenaeus, so they were pestilent heresies by then. 1 Jn.5:5-9 refutes both, saying Jesus Christ is God incarnate, not just a spirit or a man,

Internal proof: A Comma origin in the 1 John autograph of the 1st-century is verified by the following textual proofs:

1. Comma divine witness proves error of well-known 1st-century heresy.

2. Comma topics/terms are common in John's gospel & epistles.

3. There is an implied comparison of *three agree in one* outside the Comma with *three are one* in the Comma.

4. Comma portions in verses 7, 8 are authenticated by portions outside the Comma.

5. The Comma Trinity explains verse 5:7 participle masculinity, and the 5:8 Comma masculine participle is explained by the masculine deity indicated by *three agree in one*.

6. Spirit dictation of the Comma introduces the basic 3-in-1 nature of the Trinity and the image of the Trinity in Jesus Christ.

7. With the Comma present, verse 5:9 sums up verses 5:7,8

8. With the Comma present, *Spirit*, *water* and *blood* masculine-gender treatment is explained on the basis of both grammar and context parallelism.

9. Comma absence omits John's unique term *Word* for *Son*,

10. Comma absence omits *in earth* tied to the earthly nature of *Spirit*, *water* and *blood*.

11. Comma absence improperly divides a clause between two verses, as seen by the NIV and by NASV clause/verse shuffling needed to create logical syntax with the Comma absent.

12. Comma authenticity is conclusively proved by its heavenly and earthly-witness role in explaining the meaning of 1 Jn.5:6-9.

External proof: Comma continuity in Latin-church quotes dated to the early 3rd century and a mid 2nd century origin of the Italic Old Latin text, offer a potential manuscript link to the 1 John autograph.[50] This history and providential timing endowing the Received Text in a text-renewal plan of God, finalize authenticity already proven by internal evidence.

Manuscript weight

Proven Comma authenticity reveals text-criticism error in ignoring tampering. Traditional-Text minor support is attributable to many copyists in large unbiblical eastern churches often repeating limited tampering vs. a few copying the true text in small true churches. From early times, some readings likely were preserved only in true churches. And Comma Latin-church history, its presence in 10th-18th century Greek manuscripts and its wide appearance in a providentially-timed Received Text, qualify it as part of a text-renewal plan of God that defeated a history of censorship. The authenticity of the Comma illustrates the fact of God's Hand guiding chosen servants to determine content of the traditional texts of His people, and this is the final authority, not scholars' textual criticism and man's faulty hand on manuscripts.

Conclusion

No passage could have greater textual proof than the Comma, and this seems to be God's plan to inform the mind of faith when manuscript support is minimal due to satan's work. We're not to depend on self-appointed scholars who pass judgment on the text. Renewal is part of the preservation process that ensures that we can have God's inerrant Word in texts that He has ordained. We either trust God to intervene in text history to preserve His Word for His people by guiding chosen servants in handling of manuscripts, or we trust scholars who try to find truth obscured by man's faulty hand on widely variant texts, using text criticism so faulty that it's blind to evidence of tampering. To those who trust God, the Comma, the one literal scriptural testimony to the doctrine of the Trinity, is seen to be totally authentic, and inspired by the Spirit, and revealing Jesus Christ's sacred relationship in the divine Trinity guaranteeing success of his salvation mission.

End Notes on the Johannine Comma Topic

27. Dr. T. Holland. 2000. *Crowned with Glory*.
AV1611.com/kjbp/faq/Holland_1Jo5_7.html
28. Maynard, M. *A History of the Debate over 1 John 5:7-8*. p265
29. Hills, Op. Cit. p209-12.
30. Bultmann, R. 1973. *The Johannine Epistles*. Phila. Fortress Press. p81.
31. *Clarke's Commentary*. N.Y. Abingdon Cokesbury Press. p931-33.
32. Nolan, F. 1815. *An Inquiry into the Integ. of the Gr. Vulg...London*.
33 Tertullian's *one essence*, not *one person*, is the true sense of the Comma. Cyprian notes the Comma *are one*, not a suggested 1 Jn.5:8 *agree in one*. Greek for *are one* & *agree in one* differ.
34. Scrivener, F.H.A. *A Plain Introduction to N.T. Criticism*. Vo.2. p42-3.
35. Allix, P. *Remarks upon the Ecclesiastical History of the Ancient Churches of the Albigenses*. Ch.7, p51. 1989 ed. Reprint of 1821 ed
36. Kenyon, F. 1951. *Our Bible & the Ancient Manuscripts*. Harper. p169
37. Hurst, J.F. 1897. *Hist. of the Christ. Ch.*. Vol. 1. Eaton & Mains. p834
38. www.LibertyparkUSAfd.org/lp/Burgon/support.htm
39. Early lack of text punctuation/spacing won't negate vital reading sense
40. The NIV has a colon after *testify* and semicolon after *blood*, suggesting an obviously-incorrect end of a complete thought in each case. But these are commas in the Greek that function like the English. The verse 7 comma indicates a pause and continued wording that can only be that of the Johannine Comma, so the verse 8 fragment concludes the Johannine Comma, and the verse 8 comma joins this fragment to the rest of verse 8.
41. Gregory of Nazianzus, *Oration 32*. Para.19 Some say that in 390 A.D. Gregory defended 1 Jn.5:7,8 grammar without noting the Comma, so they say it's not original. But, with the Comma present, there's no grammar issue, so the contest indicates Comma involvement. Some in that day said grammar in Gregory's text was faulty, and the likely reason is Comma exclusion, part of censorship indicated by others.
42. A theory that the 5:7 participle ties to 5:9 *men* is unlikely. Here there's simply a contrast of any witness of men with that of God in the Trinity and Jesus' person, by the Comma. Summing-up of the Trinity witness and earthly witness in Jesus is the topic. (Wallace, D. *Greek Grammar and the Personality of the Holy Spirit*. Bltn. for Bib. Res. 13.1. 2003. 97-125).
43. Dr. Thomas Strouse. *Refutation of Dr. Daniel Wallaces's Rejection of the KJV as the Best Translation*. www.Emmanuel-Newington.org/Seminary/Resources/Refutation

44. Marshall, I.H. 1978. *The Epistles of John*. Eerdmans. p237. Imposed masculine sense on *blood/water* by a tie to natural-masculine *Spirit* is credible, but uncertain, and lack of imposed natural masculinity on the 5:6 participle by *Spirit* argues against it. Masculine sense imposed on neuter terms by a tie to one natural-masculine term isn't as credible as a masculine sense of all three terms individually related to *Father, Word, Holy Ghost*.

45. *dia* with genitive *water/blood* in the 5:6 first clause, is *through* in the sense of, *by means of* (gen. of means). The same sense applies at 1 Jn.4:9.

46. . *The New Testament in the Original Greek*. Vol 2. London. MacMillan. 1881. p277-82.

47. Bednar, L. *Evidence of the Divine Hand on True Scripture*. p203-04.

48 *Comments on the Received Text of F. Scrivener*.www.wcBible.org

49. Bednar, Op. Cit. The entire book deals with inerrancy.

50.The mid-2nd century Italic is close to autographs, and underlying Greek is closer still. Comma references (not always exact, but clear) in Latin church history reveal its acceptance throughout this history: i.e. Tertullian in 215 A.D, Cyprian 258, Idacius Clarus 350, Priscillian 385, Cassian 435, Carthage council 484, Cassiodorus 580, Old Latin texts Wianburgensis, r and Speculum of 5-8th centuries, Vulgate ~800 A.D and 13th-15th century Waldensen versions. This partial listing, supported by Athanasius (4th century Greek church) and Greek 10th-18th century manuscripts, indicates Latin-church continuity of Comma acceptance from the start, with Greek-church support (N.T. texts all lack major extant pre-200 A.D. evidence).

The Italic text differs from faulty Old Latin texts of poor translators. Augustine said *Now among the translations themselves the Italian (Italic) is to be preferred to the others*, for it keeps closer to the words without prejudice to clarity of expression. *Metzger, B.M. 1977*. The Early Versions of the N.T. Clarendon. p290-93. He also said of the Itala (Italic), *which is more faithful in its renderings and more intelligible in its sense*. Nicol, T. 1915. The Old Latin Versions. International Standard Bible Encyclopedia.

Authenticity: Calvary Theology in a Seeming Contradiction

The Crucifixion hour
Mark
15:25 *And it was the <u>third</u> hour, and they crucified him.*
John
19:14 *And it was the preparation of the passover, and about the*
<u>sixth</u> hour: and he saith unto the Jews, Behold your king!
19:15 *But they cried out, Away with him…crucify him…*
19:16 *Then delivered he him therefore unto them to be*
crucified…

Daylight hours began at 6:00 AM, so the 3rd hour ended at 9:00 AM, and the 6th at 12 noon. The Crucifixion began at the 3rd hour, as in Mark. Luke/Matthew support this, noting Crucifixion events preceding the 6th hour, soldiers offering Jesus vinegar (Lk. 23:36), and crucified thieves railing on Him (Lk.23:39, Mt.27: 44). And sun-darkening occurred at the 6th hour (Mt.27:45, Lk. 23:44), well after the Crucifixion began. So why does Jn.19:14 say the Crucifixion began about the 6th hour? It's said the 6th-hour is the Roman 6 AM, three hours before the Crucifixion, but John uses the same daylight hours other gospel writers use (In Jn. 1:39 the day nears an end at about the 10th hour, or 4 PM).

Jn.19:14 says, *And it* (Crucifixion day) *was the preparation of the Passover.* Crucifixion day was a preparation day when the Passover lamb is slain, which is the day before Passover day. And Mt.27:62, Mk.15:42 and Lk.23:54 all say Crucifixion day was a preparation day. All four gospels show Christ crucified on a Passover preparation day when the sacrificial lamb was slain. In this He superseded and replaced the Passover sacrifice and became the ultimate sacrifice to establish a New Testament order.

But to supersede old Passover, He first had to relate to it, doing so in a first old Passover with His disciples the day <u>before the Crucifixion</u>. This was followed by the first New Passover observance (Communion), tying Christ to the old and new.

The gospels reveal two old Passover days in Jerusalem, and they aren't discordant accounts of one. As noted, all the gospels say Christ was crucified the day before a Passover supper day, and Lk.22:7-20, Mt.26:17-29 and Mk.14:12-25 note another Passover supper Christ and His disciples observed on the <u>day before the Crucifixion</u>. This latter was on a first day of unleavened bread in Passover week. The day begins at evening after the lamb-slaying preparation. It continues until the next evening, so Christ and His disciples observed a first Passover, and He was crucified the next morning ~9:00 AM on the same Passover day. Thus a latter part of first Passover day was Crucifixion Day and preparation day for another Passover day soon to begin that evening (Jn.19:31), tying Christ to both old Passovers. He died near 3:00 PM (Lk.23:44-46), the time when the killing of Passover lambs began. His body was taken off the cross before second Passover day began.

In summary Christ superseded old Passover by relating to it, then following this with the first new one to declare the superseding Passover. He finalized and fulfilled the matter by His sacrifice on the Cross at preparation time for the second old Passover day. The second old Passover took on a new significance as Christ became God's ultimate Passover (1 Cor.5:7), as we'll see.

Now why were there two Passover days? Mt.27:62, Lk.23:54, Mk.15:42 & Jn.19:31 all say the day after the Crucifixion was a Sabbath. Saturday after Crucifixion Friday was both a weekly and a Passover Sabbath. Passover Sabbath began at evening at 6 PM Friday the solar day, as John 19:31 notes, calling the Sabbath soon to begin that Friday evening a *high day*. This contrasts with weekly Sabbath day that began the next morning at the 1st hour at 6:00 AM, as seen by the Mt.28:1...*in the end of the Sabbath as it began to dawn toward the first day of the week* (Sunday). Thus weekly Saturday Sabbath ended at morning as Sunday began (Berry's Interlinear wrongly renders *dusk*, for *dawn* is correct in this context, as even modern versions say). Jews utilized Passover time with a full day starting at 6 PM, and daylight hours starting at 6 AM, as in gospel Crucifixion/Resurrection accounts.

At the subject Passover, two overlapping Sabbath days created one extending from 6PM Friday to 6AM Sunday. A Sabbath work-prohibition problem results, work on preparation day (Crucifixion Friday) being required of the people. If Passover and weekly Sabbath days are separated, work-prohibition time is clear. With no separation, the two time frames overlap, and the two days join in an extended observance. Thus the days lose, in part, individual identities (like Siamese twins sharing a body part). Now, weekly Sabbath work-prohibition includes a period of 6PM Friday to 6AM Saturday, and Passover Sabbath work-prohibition includes a period of 6PM Saturday to 6AM Sunday. Each Sabbath is unique, the weekly honoring God's rest from creation and the Passover His deliverance of Israel from Egypt. The Sabbaths become an unorthodox joint observance of two days individually important to the Jews. At some point, perhaps not long before the Crucifixion, priests would view preparation day as a problem when the two Sabbaths overlapped.

Sabbath work-prohibition emphasis during Jesus' ministry indicates work-prohibition times would be of great concern. But with overlapping Sabbaths, is work-prohibition governed by time limits of Passover or weekly Sabbath? If the prohibition begins Friday evening, as in evening-to-evening Passover Sabbath, the sense of morning-to-morning weekly Sabbath is lost. If it ends Sunday morning, as in morning-to-morning weekly Sabbath, the sense of evening-to-evening Passover Sabbath is lost. In a combined Sabbath, does Passover-Sabbath work-prohibition extend to Friday morning and does weekly Passover-Sabbath work-prohibition extend to Sunday evening? Time limits of the events are mixed, and neither can take precedence, both being important.

A logical solution is to institute an early second Passover day in Jerusalem in a 48-hour two-part old Passover. The people observe early Passover from 6PM Thursday to 6PM Friday, then weekly Sabbath from 6AM Saturday to 6AM Sunday, avoiding all suggestion of Sabbath work. Priests and Levites normally do

Sabbath work and observe a regular 6PM Friday to 6PM Saturday Passover day, then a 6PM Saturday to 6AM Sunday weekly Sabbath. The first observance for the people is the one Christ observed before the Crucifixion. Passover in Mt.26, Mk.14 and Lk.22 deals only with the people, mainly the disciples, and that of Jn.18:28 appears to deal only with priests and their associates.

This approach to the problem is natural. In locales far from Jerusalem a dual Passover was observed due to lunar calendar variance and no Jerusalem input on the right day. And it accords with Sabbath work-prohibition zeal seen during Jesus' ministry. And Pharisees would favor a special Passover, being famous for such things, their *fence around the law* being an elaborate system of their own rules designed to prevent violation of the law.

A priests' Passover day fits with Christ's exclusive high priest status. Once a year, in the temple Holy of Holies, the old high priest sought God's intervention for the nation, and other priests had supportive roles. Christ provided the sacrifice for priests to make them one with the people before God. He ended the levitical priesthood as the Holy-of-Holies veil rent in two at the time of His death in sacrifice for all, and the way to God the Father was opened to all believers. The high priest's ministry in representing God's people to the Father transferred to Christ, and individual access to the Father by Christ ended human priestly mediation. Christians are priests in a spiritual sense (Heb.13:15-16, 1 Tim. 2:5). God marked the end of the levitical priesthood by temple destruction in 70 A.D, after which rabbinical Judaism began.

John notes the first 24-hour day, extending from 6PM Thursday to 6PM Friday, in terms of the 48-hour day of 6PM Thursday to 6PM Saturday. He doubles the Friday 3rd hour of other gospels to represent the 48-hour day as a 24-hour day (48 hours superimpose on a 24-hour day to double hours). This relates to Jesus' identification with old Passover day in a first observance and His sacrifice on preparation day of the second to create one New Passover day superseding the old in fulfilling its typology. The two days revert to one symbolically as the first old Passover ties to the second so that the second presents Christ's sacrifice as God's ultimate Passover for Israel (the priests' day honors the ultimate high priest). John's 6th hour portrays the 48-hour event, consisting of one Passover for the people and one for priests, as reverting to one day for the people and priests in Christ's one Passover day for all. The New Testament era formally began as the New Passover fulfilled old Passover typology and eternal life was affirmed by the Resurrection for or all who trust in Christ.

God's Promise of Eternal Preservation of His Word: Ps. 12

KJB
1. *Help Lord; for the godly man ceaseth; for the faithful fail...*
2. *They speak vanity every one with his neighbor: with flattering lips and with a double heart do they speak.*
3. *The Lord shall cut off all flattering lips, and the tongue that speaketh proud things:*
4. *Who have said, With our tongue will we prevail; our lips are our own: who is lord over us?*
5. *For the oppression of the poor, for the sighing of the needy, now will I arise, saith the Lord; I will set him in safety from him that puffeth at him.*
6. *The words of the Lord are pure words: as silver tried in a furnace of earth, purified seven times.*
7. *Thou shalt keep them O Lord, thou shalt preserve them from this generation for ever* (to eternity).
8. *The wicked walk on every side when the vilest men are exalted.*

NASV
(5) *Now I will arise, "says the Lord; "I will set him in the safety for which he longs." (6) The words of the Lord are pure words...(7) Thou O Lord, wilt keep them. Thou wilt preserve him from this generation forever.*

NIV
(5) *I will now arise," says the Lord. "I will protect them from those who malign them. (6) And the words of the Lord are flawless...(7). O Lord you Will keep us safe and protect us from such people forever.*

The KJB 12:5 says of the oppressed godly man...*saith the Lord, I will set him in safety*...12:6 says God's words are pure (true), and 12:7 says He keeps (performs) them forever. Deliverance of the godly is stressed, but that's the object of God's words, and the main emphasis is on what *saith the Lord*, His *words* promising deliverance. 12:7 stresses God keeping and preserving *them*, His words <u>certifying</u> His care of the righteous, not just in David's time, but forever. The declared eternal preservation stresses His written words certifying deliverance of the righteous forever.

It's said 12:7 *them* is 12:5 people, but *them* loses its sure sense if separated from its 12:6 immediate antecedent *words* (12:6 shifts emphasis from people to *words*). If people were meant, the text would distort pronoun reference. Those proposing people dismiss the antecedent factor, saying gender discord denies *words* [12:7 *them* (verb suffix) is masculine, and 12:6 *words* (substantive) is feminine]. Hebrew pronouns and antecedents usually agree in gender, but Gesenius says *masculine suffixes (especially in the <u>plural</u>) are not infrequently used to refer to* feminine *subtantives*.[49] Waltke & O'Connor say, *The masculine pronoun is often used for a feminine antecedent*.[50] Strouse notes normal gender discord in Ps.119:111,129,152,167, God's Words, *testimonies* (f) linking to *they/them* (m),[51] which to the present writer is gender discord by design[52] tying our need of God's Word for sustenance (f) to His power as provider (m). More examples of designed gender discord are Ex.1:21 *midwives*, Gn.26:15 *wells* [f] and Isa. 3:16 *daughters* that are all antecedents to a masculine *them*.

Hebrew gender discord is common, but antecedent discord is not, as needed to avoid much confusion of sense. And passage sense takes priority over grammar issues like gender discord,[50] and Ps.12:6,7 sense ties *them* to *words* in the immediate context.

In Psalms poetry parallelism, a theme repeats in related wording, and 12:7 repeats a 12:6 theme on purity of God's words. 12:6 likens the purity to that of truly refined silver to stress that they aren't idle words, but pure ones that will be <u>kept</u>. The initial 12:7

clause repeats the theme, stressing God's word-keeping to link 12:7 *them* to 12:6 *words*, and they (2nd *them*) are preserved forever to signify being kept forever. 12:7 further stresses purity of words kept by God by making *Thou* in the first clause a separate word in Hebrew, a device for emphasis, *thou* normally being limited to a prefix on a Hebrew imperfect verb here (KJB *Thou & O Lord* in the first clause retain the emphasis in English style). The major purity theme relates directly to God's words, His people being the objects of His pure words (Eph.5:26, Jn.15:3).

Word-keeping emphasis grows as Hebrew-text gender discord by design ties *them* to *words*. A masculine pronoun and feminine antecedent reflects Hebrew use of masculine gender to signify power, and feminine to signify compassion.[53] Ps.12:6,7 ties masculine *them* to feminine *words*, relating almighty God's power to keep *them* to His compassion (noted in 12:5) applying the power (similar to Hebrew prior-gender masculine language inclusive of both natural genders - e.g. the Ps.12 godly man includes men & women).[54] And in compassion God preserves His words forever to certify that He obligates Himself to keep them forever.[55]

An initial NASV *them* suggests *words*, but *him* for the next *them* implies people as objects of preserving; they're objects of word-keeping, so teaching on words certifying man's deliverance is lost. And *him* ties to *them*, mixing the singular and plural in ambiguity of sense (here *them* can be *words* or people). Actually *him*, good Hebrew, is bad English; this 3rd-person/singular/masculine pronoun signifies, not people, but 3rd-person/singular/masculine *word*. Hebrew lacks neuter gender, *him* often signifying neuter terms called *it / that* in English (e.g. in Nu.22:20 God speaks, the Hebrew saying, *the word that I shall speak to you, him* (*it / that*) *you shall do.*[56] Ps.12:7 Hebrew says, *Thou shalt keep thy words* (*them*) *O Lord, thou shalt preserve thy word. Thy word* is *thy words*, and *them* rightly signifies *word*, *it / that* being awkward and confusing. Psalms number discord, usually for poetic style, is didactic here, stressing God's written words preserved forever.

Words is spoken or written scripture, but *word* stresses the written (God's *word* is His written *words*). His words preserved for us require the written form, preserved forever to show He <u>obligates Himself</u> to keep them forever (by the *Living Word*). The KJB second *them* doesn't lose the purpose of the text shift to *him*, declared eternal preservation (for us) establishing the written form.

The NIV, like the extant Septuagint, has a wrong *us* for the 12:7 double *them*. *Us*, wrong by definition in the first use and pointing in the second, makes people objects of keeping and preserving, when they're objects only of <u>word</u>-keeping. *Us* can't fit passage sense unless language is altered, and *such people* serves only to justify *us*. The two terms mask interpretation nonsense resulting if *them* were people, a sense of eternal preservation of godly men from one generation of evil men of David's time that can't live forever. This sense would be invoked by using *us* in conjunction with a correct *this generation*, making the incorrect *such people* necessary. Linguistic error of this approach further shows *such people* is poor, *from* people being poor language; *this generation* is that of David and joins *from* with *to/for* to note a period <u>from</u> that time <u>to</u> eternity (the Hebrew says this), or <u>for</u> ever. And *this* acts as a relative pronoun,[57] so *such* is poor; i.e. we read *from the generation <u>this</u> (which) is to forever*, not *from the generation such is to forever.* But eternal preservation of words in God's written Word is fully logical, with no linguistic problem or faulty sense.

Scholars say the true text is scattered in manuscripts, and that they must identify it (ensures error). They say Ps.119:89 *For ever O Lord thy word is settled in heaven* means preservation is realized only in heaven. But the sense of the Hebrew is that preservation is controlled and verified in heaven where there's no confusion. Context supports this, earthly preservation being why the writer can obey God's testimonies (119:88) and why earth endures by God's law (119:91). Ps.119:96 notes an end, or a limit, to earthly perfection, but calls God's commandments (to us) *exceeding broad*, unlimited perfection, so His Word to us is fully preserved.

End Notes on the Word-Preservation Topic

49. *Gesenius' Heb. Gram..* 2nd English Ed, Cowley, A.E. 1910. Para.135o.

50 Waltke, B.K. & O'Connor, M.P. 1990. *An Introduction to Biblical Hebrew Syntax.* Eisenbraums. Winona Lake, IN. #16.4b, p302.

51. Strouse, T.M. *A Critique of "God's Word in Our Hands:" The Bible Preserved for Us.* The Burning Bush. 11/1 June 2005. p28

52. Gesenius, Op. Cit. para. 110k.

53. Gesenius, Op. Cit. paragraph 122h – see footnote #3

54. Gesenius, Op. Cit. para.122g

55. It's said chiasmus-inversion parallelism ties 12:5 & 7 of like content on the godly man, separated by a dissimilar 12:6 on God's Words. That's unlikely due to resultant pronoun ambiguity, and style isolation of 12: 5-7 from the rest of the Psalm, and language too dissimilar to link separated verses this way. Dissimilarity includes, mismatch of 12:5 *him* to the first 12:7 *them*, different 12:5 & 7 speakers, 12:5 *him* protected once but 12:7 *them* kept & preserved and no reference to God's arising and its cause in 12:7 or to generation/eternality aspects in 12:5. And the proposed inversion doesn't apply to any of the evident Psalm 12 parallelisms noted below.

Couplet-clause parallelism in each verse of the Psalm offers no possibility of the inversion, and couplet-verse parallelism in the entire Psalm states action and the reason for it, offering no possibility of the inversion.

Psalm 12 chiastic cause/effect contrasting verse pairs (1/8; 2,3/6,7; 4/5) isolate 12:5 & 7. Verses 2,3 pair with 6,7 and contain 2,6 & 3,7 contrasting pairs. 12:1 notes a cause of trouble for the godly, and 12:8 notes a potential evil end effect. 12:2,3 expound the cause of trouble, evil men's impure/vain/temporal intent to harm the godly, in contrast with a 12:6,7 effect of God's pure/reliable/eternal promise to defend the godly. In 12:4 evil ones intend to act, saying *We will*, causing a 12:5 contrast of God saying, *No, I will*.

In summary, poetic style isolates 12:5 & 7 to deny *them* is people. It ties gender discordant *them* & *words*, the 12:5 godly man (m) being delivered by God's 12:6 words of compassion (f), and 12:7 *them* being words also of power (m) to deliver. And 12:5 & 7 differ by speaker & pronoun number to deny a link in a common reference to people, but 12:6 & 12:7 link *words* to *them* in both ways to affirm a reference to *words*.

56. Other NASV *him/he* error is, *safety for which he longs*. The sense of the Hebrew is the KJB *puffeth* (NIV agrees), a blast of evil men's breath.

57. Gesenius said the Masora teaches this. Op. Cit. para. 126y

66

Authenticity: God-Guided Translation

1. Prophecy fulfillment seen only in the KJB, while inerrancy is retained, would be evidence of KJB providential guidance, and this occurs in Genesis. Some evolutionists propose a millions-of-years gap from Gen.1:1 to 1:2 in which man-like beings lived and perished, saying the KJB 1:28 *replenish the earth* means Adam was to repopulate the earth. But *replenish* meant *fill* in 1611 England (*replete* is still *filled*), and the translators didn't know of the future *refill* sense. Use in a refill sense occurred ~1 year after KJB publication, in poetry that distorts literality, and it occurred sporadically later (Oxford Eng. Dict), not being established until over 200 years later, still meaning *fill* in Webster's 1828 dictionary.[58]

Use of *replenish* in Genesis is unique. In view of the *refill* sense applying long after 1611, the 1:28 command to replenish can be seen as signifying veiled prophecy on earth's population loss in Gen.9:1 after the flood to fulfill 1:28 prophecy. That is, God spoke to Adam on filling the earth, and prophesied to Noah in Adam's loins on refilling it after the flood (similar to Heb.7:10 where Levi in Abraham's loins pays tithes to Melchisedec).

KJB translators unknowingly linked *replenish* in Gen.9:1 and 1:28, making these the only uses in Genesis and linking creation to the great flood.[59] They rendered Hebrew for *replenish, fill* in a 1:22 command in the same context as 1:28, on fish not fully destroyed in the flood and <u>not in need of refilling</u>. This Hebrew is used in like sense in 7 other Genesis verses, and they rendered it *fill*, not *replenish*, and *refill* can't apply. How can this be when they did not differentiate *fill* and *replenish*? It appears God guided them by a need to replace antiquated *plenish* (fill) with *replenish*, English versions consulted providentially placing *plenish* where *replenish* later would substitute, and much later would mean *refill* (God's work, for no version writer knew the future). KJB translators

---

<u>58</u>. Daniels, D.W. 2002. Chick Publications web site on Bible versions.
<u>59</u>. The water-vapor canopy placed above the firmament in creation is a source of 40-day rain of the flood, so God foretells the flood at creation.

67

would be aware only of a textual item, but 9:1 fulfilling of 1:28 prophecy, <u>visible only in the KJB and long after 1611</u>, reveals God's hand in arranging a textual item. *Replenish*, marking God's hand on the text, must be retained, and the 1769 edition providentially ended KJB language up-dating that alters such words.[60]

<u>2</u>. **Mt.14:18/Lk.7:20**: A plan of God revealed only in the KJB, as text inerrancy is retained, will reveal KJB providential guidance, which occurs in Mt.14/Lk.7. Evidently God signified the end of the Old Testament era in a way giving precedence to the New, as indicated by criticism of the KJB for making John's baptizer role a last name. Lk.7:20 says *John Baptist*; Mt.14:8 says *John Baptist's head*...Now to say *John the Baptist* can't be *John Baptist* is to say *Jesus the Christ* can't be *Jesus Christ*. *Christ* and *Baptist* are roles that become names.[61] *Jesus Christ* is equivalent to *Jesus the Christ*, as *John Baptist* is equivalent to *John the Baptist*.

In both verses the Greek reads *John the Baptist*, as the KJB has it usually, but can be the equivalent *John Baptist*. It's in two gospels and relates to the same event in both, John's imprisonment and death (He's in prison in Mt.11:2 and so during his disciples' Lk.7:20 discourse with Christ). The matter is of deliberate design.

Context specifies *John Baptist* in the two verses. Jesus Christ and John brought in the New Testament era (John prepared the way, introducing Christ by miraculous birth partly reflecting the Virgin Birth, and by baptism of Jesus in Jordan, and he preached and baptized for repentance crucial to salvation). But John's work was soon to end at the time of the Mt.14 / Lk.7 event; as the last Old Testament prophet, his death ended Old Testament ties to the work. *Jesus Christ* signifies Jesus the Christ, the anointed Savior whose death and resurrection began the New Testament era. And *John Baptist* signifies John the baptizer, the role of the last pro-

---

60. By this Providence, other old words that can be up-dated aren't, older English being more suitable than ever-degenerating modern English.

61. More examples: *Simon Zelotes* signifies *Simon the zealot*, avid follower & *Mary Magdalene* signifies *Mary the Magdalene*, resident of Magdala.

phet whose death ended the Old Testament era (he said of Christ, *He must increase, but I must decrease* - Jn.3:30). John is a unique Old Testament prophet, for, while others like Moses and Isaiah foretold Christ, John introduced Him. *John Baptist* identifies him, by the role, with *Jesus Christ* in bringing in the New Testament era (they were even kinsmen by the earthly tie). The tie is also seen in that, as Jesus had God's Spirit beyond measure (Jn.3:34), John was filled by God's Spirit from before birth (Lk.1:15). And the Malachi 4:2 *Sun of righteousness* with healing in his wings is Christ, while the Malachi 4:5 *Elijah* introducing the day of the Lord is John in association with Christ [First & Second Advents are noted in Malachi, with Elijah-type John at the First Advent (Mt.17:9-12) and the literal Elijah at the Second (Rev.11:3)].

A *John Baptist* tie to *Jesus Christ* signifies the end of the Old Testament era at John's death, giving precedence to the New soon to begin with Jesus' death and resurrection. Death ends the Old era, but Resurrection victory over death begins the better New era. God's guidance by KJB-translator recognition of veiled contextual sense controls the rendering, to tie John's Old Testament status to his New Testament baptizer role. John's forerunner baptism of repentance in death to self-desire, the final Old-Testament one, is superseded by Christ's baptism of the Spirit (Ro.6:4) signifying death to the entire old man and resurrection to new life. This reflects John's death and superseding of the Old Testament era by Christ and the Resurrection life of the New Testament era.

3. Providential Guidance & a theophany of Christ: Dan. 3:25
It's said Nebuchadnezzar, in Dan.3:25 Aramaic, called a 4th figure in his furnace *a son of the gods*, not the KJV *the Son of God*, since Aramaic *elahin* is *gods*; KJV translators knew it's usually *gods* (Dan.2:11,47; 4:8,9,18; 5:4,11,14,23), but made an exception. In Aramaic construct grammar *the* gods (Babylon's gods) requires *the* son, and the king earlier recognized Daniel's one *God of gods* (Dan.2:47), so *the Son of God* is valid. He said, *the son of the gods*, but saw *the gods* as his God, now ruled by a supreme God, and

the son of (this) God relates to Christ subtly. And *God of gods* of a prophetic dream God gave the king, relates to revelation given to him on an eternal kingdom of God/Christ (Dan.2:44). And a sense of *the Son of God* as Christ in theophany attaches to *the son of the gods*; that is, *the gods* diminish in the king's eyes, due to both a *God of gods* and *the son of the gods* (the latter signifies the Son of God as truth born anew out of lesser faith in *gods*).

The king's *the son of the gods* in Aramaic of Babylon, would read that way to Babylonians. Hebrews would read plural *elahin* as their plural *Elohim* that usually refers to the one true God (the Trinity likely), and would read *the Son of the God* or *the Son of God*. Babylonians read as they're meant to, and Hebrews read a higher Messianic sense as they're meant to. Daniel Aramaic deals with speakings or acts of Babylonians, for historical authenticity, and the Masoretic Text speaks inerrantly to two different cultures.

In Dan.3:28 Nebuchadnezzar interprets, calling the 4th figure an angel (his idea of *Son*; an angel is *a son*) of God (*a son of God* saved Daniel from lions & *the Son of God* saved three from the fire, Christology being involved in the latter case). The king did not know of Christ, but a sense of Christ in theophany ties to *the son of the gods*, initially for Hebrew Christology mystery, and later for translations in true churches over the centuries. KJV translation, inerrant by construct grammar and context, preserves the right term. The NKJV has this term, but equivocates with an incorrect footnote alternative, *a son of the gods* applying only to unbiblical culture. Other modern versions have incorrect *a son of the gods* in the text. *The Son of God* is in very old texts likely tied to the apostolic era,[62] and the KJV preserves truth likely given to original biblical churches, but modern versions lose this.

---

62. Syriac Peshitta of early origin (see Lamsa) & Vulgate, likely from its Old Latin Italic basis dated to the 2nd century, suggesting early eastern & western biblical churches read *the Son of God*. Athanasius, early eastern church (died 373 A.D.), quoted Dan.3:25, the *Son of God* (*Four Discourses against the Arians*. 4:24. www.mb-soft.com/believe/txuc/Athana43.htm).

4. Providential Guidance: Jesus Gives Rest to God's people

Again the KJB reveals a theophany of Christ missed by modern scholars. Using His incarnate name, the KJB Heb.4:8 places Him with Hebrew wilderness wanderers after the exodus. It's no surprise to see Christ here, for Micah 5:2 says He took on humanity at Bethlehem as the eternal God *whose goings forth* (activities) *have been from of old, from everlasting* (no beginning of days – note: modern-version *ancient* in lieu of *everlasting* is erroneous).

The KJB Heb.4:8 notes Jesus not giving the Hebrew wilderness wanderers a spiritual rest in faith. Early church elders understood the passage to refer to Christ,[63] but today scholars don't. Greek for Jesus (*Iesous*) transliterates and corresponds to Joshua's Hebrew name (*Yeshua*), so Modern versions mistakenly present historical Joshua as the Jesus of the verse, suggesting Joshua led his people to eventual rest in Canaan, people whose faithlessness points to a greater spiritual rest of faith for God's people.[64]

Hebrew names in the New Testament Greek form don't apply here. The Greek text is inspired, so *Iesous* in Hebrews can't be Joshua, for that creates identity confusion denying inerrancy, there being no qualifying explanation. If historical Joshua had been intended, he'd be identified in a way other than a name transliteration. This is likely, for the scholarly Hebrews writer, an expert in Hebrew culture and Greek language, would see the ambiguity and potential for misconstruing a Greek transliteration.

And the name Jesus signifying Christ is noted shortly after verse 8, in verse 14, and rest in verse 8 relates to the verse 14-16 theme on God's mercy and grace as the basis for rest. The epistle concentrates on Christ, *Jesus* referring to Christ throughout (2:9, 6:20, 7:22, 10:19, 12:2,24 & 13:12), while Joshua is nowhere evident and can't be abruptly introduced in 4:8.

63. Evans, C.A. 2002. *The Scriptures of Jesus and His Earliest Followers.* "The Canon Debate." Ed. Mcdonald, L.M. & Sanders, J.A.
64. Hagner, D.A. 1983. *Hebrews: A Good News Commentary.* San Fran. Harper & Row. p51

That Heb.4:8 refers to Joshua is contextually and linguistically unsound, as seen by further indication of Christ here in Israel's past. The verse is preceded by chapters 3,4 on failure of Moses-led wanderers to enter a rest of faith in God. This spiritual rest is the only type referenced in Heb.4:8. The rest scripture relates Joshua to, by his leadership in Canaan victories, was a physical one, and while Heb.4:8 may imply the physical, it doesn't refer to Joshua. The physical rest was given by God through Christ, as seen by Christ appearing in theophany as *Captain of the Host* before whom Joshua bowed in submission before deciding Israel's actions (Jos.5:13-15). Thus even an implied reference to physical rest would be to Christ, and this Jesus is the one who didn't give the greater spiritual rest. Accordingly the pronoun *he* in Heb.4:8 refers to Christ, as expected with *Jesus* being the immediate grammatical antecedent, while scholars link *he* to a grammatically-distant reference to God the Father.

With Jesus giving physical rest, language/context prove Christ is the Heb.4:7,8 Jesus. The KJV says, *Again, he limiteth a certain day, saying in David, To day, after so long a time...harden not your hearts...if Jesus had given them rest* (can imply physical rest by Jesus, but use of *Joshua* exceeds context) *then would he not afterward have spoken of another day*. When *he* spoke of another day of rest, this was *in* (through) David at the writing of Ps.95, ~400 years after the time of historical Joshua. How can this Joshua be with wilderness wanderers and ~400 years later be alive to speak in/through David? And how can he speak *in David*, speaking holy scripture? But Jesus Christ, the eternal living Word of God, has no trouble being with the wilderness wanderers, and 400 years later speaking scripture through David.

NIV/RSV translators justify *Joshua* in this passage, changing *he* (God the Son) to *God* (the Father implied). This permits a change in passage sense that allows the name of historic Joshua linguistically (but not contextually). But the RSV reveals in footnotes, that the Greek says *he*, not *God*, and the Amplified and NASV render *he*. The NASV tries to skirt the issue, capitalizing *H* in *he* to suggest God the Father or Jesus can be understood. Jewett in a personal translation, with no group pressure, renders *he* and notes the impossibility that *Jesus* could be the historical Joshua.[65]

The Hebrews writer relates Christ's role in dealing with lack of faith of God's Old Testament people at a time in history when the presence of Christ is verified in 1 Cor.10:4. Paul calls Christ the spiritual rock that followed Israel (in the wilderness wandering with Israel under Moses). A major purpose of the Hebrews writer is to relate Jesus, not Joshua, to Old Testament history, and Heb. 4:8 does so. He teaches Mic.5:2 truth on activities of Christ that pre-date His Incarnation at Bethlehem and illustrate His status as God without beginning of days. Modern scholars miss the intent of the writer to give truth on activities of Christ preincarnate.

5. Providential Guidance: Jesus Leads God's Old Testament people. Another case of *Jesus*/Joshua is the Acts 7 encounter of Stephen the Christian martyr with the Jerusalem council. In the KJB Stephen notes ancient Hebrew fathers bringing in the tabernacle <u>with Jesus</u> into Canaan. In the NASV/RSV, they bring in the tabernacle <u>with Joshua</u>, which is awkward and ambiguous; it can be logically interpreted as saying the fathers acted with Joshua to bring the tabernacle into Canaan, but can be illogically interpreted as saying the fathers brought in the tabernacle and their leader Joshua together. In the NIV the problem is handled by saying the tabernacle was brought in <u>under</u> Joshua's leadership, an inaccuracy obscuring the issue to allow *Joshua*.

But *Jesus* offers dual-sense logic, not ambiguity, suggesting more than one truth and indicating *Jesus* is correct. This logic has both physical and spiritual aspects. In a physical sense the fathers act with Jesus, the Captain of the host and true leader, to bring in the

<u>65</u>. Jewett, R. 1981. *Letter to Pilgrims. A Commentary on the Epistle to the Hebrews.* N.Y. Pilgrim Press. p2

tabernacle to Canaan. In a spiritual sense they bring in the tabernacle and Jesus together, for the tabernacle is symbolic of Christ in several ways as any Pentateuch-class student knows.

The dual-sense logic is vital to Stephen who recounts Israel's history to the council to show them Jesus as the God of their history and denounce their crucifixion of their own Messiah (Acts 7:52). The council knows Jesus is the Messiah (Mt.21:38) and scripture can convict them of their betrayal. And Stephen knows scripture and would not miss the chance to stir up the council's scriptural knowledge by showing them dual-sense logic of Jesus spiritually associated with the tabernacle and Captain of the Host (not Joshua) giving ancient Israel physical victories in Canaan. Indeed it would be Stephen's purpose to show them it was really Jesus who gave the victories to correct their traditional belief that Joshua did this. Thus he can't mean Joshua when he says *Jesus*, for this would reverse and defeat his whole intent. He must begin to name Jesus the Christ openly at, or very near, the point of Acts 7:45 in his oration since he has only alluded to Him so far (Acts 7:37). The opportunity will soon be gone as he is very close to the point where he will denounce the council for betraying Jesus.

6. Providential Guidance: Who is the Morning Star? Isa.14:4, 12-15 Translator grasp of Hebrew word-sense is distorted at times by inadequate knowledge of ancient terminology and lexicons reliant on commentator opinion.

KJB...*take up this proverb against the king of Babylon...How art thou fallen from heaven, <u>O Lucifer, son of the morning</u>...For thou hast said in thine heart, I will ascend into heaven. I will exalt my throne above the stars of God...I will be like the most High. Yet thou shalt be brought down to <u>hell</u>...*

NIV...*take up this taunt against the king of Babylon...How you have fallen from heaven, <u>O morning star, son of the dawn</u>...You said in your heart, I will ascend to heaven; I will raise my throne above the stars of God...I will make myself like the Most High. But you are brought down to the <u>grave</u>...*

74

Isaiah 14 refers to Satan as the archangel Lucifer who wants equality with God and is cast out of heaven and ultimately into hell. This accords with Lk.10:18 where Christ says He beheld satan fall from heaven, so lucifer cast out of heaven was satan.

But the NIV *grave* in lieu of *hell*, makes the final abode for an earthly man and removes reference to Satan. Reference to Lucifer is removed, and *morning star* is assigned as a figurative name for a verse-4 earthly king of Babylon who is supposedly the subject of verses 12-14. But this makes a king of Babylon *fall from heaven* when Christ says in Lk.10:18 it was satan. Scholars think *fall from heaven* is figurative language on the king's demise, but Lk.10:18 language is literal, so the scholar view suggests a very unlikely earthly king's desire to be equal with God. That ambition characterizes Satan, and while the language may signify antichrist as the king, he's just a stand-in for Satan.

Modern scholars miss the fact that Isaiah 14 does what Psalms does at times regarding prophecy. A Psalms text may abruptly change from speaking of David's trials to prophesying parallel trials of the Son of David, Jesus Christ. In parallel, but opposite, manner, Isaiah 14 abruptly changes from speaking of an earthly king of Babylon to Satan, the spiritual kindred of this king. This also occurs in Ezk.28:11-19 regarding the king of Tyrus.

Early church elders evidently understood the parallelism, but modern scholars miss it, saying *Lucifer* is not Satan.[66,67] Thus the Satan's identity as Lucifer, lost in the NIV, is replaced by a title related here to the descriptive *morning*. Scholars justify *morning star*, as the Hebrew might be translated that way at times, but not when it's a <u>title</u>. The notion that Isa.14:12 speaks of the *morning star* is just Westcott and Hort dogma of their 1881 English Revised Version, perhaps following dogma of other commentators.

<u>66</u>. *Intl. Bible Commentary*. 1985. Ed. F.F. Bruce. N.Y. Guideposts. p732
<u>67</u>. *Harpers Dict.of the Bible*. 1985. Ed. P.J.Achtemeier. S. Fran. p582.

The problem here is that the title *morning star* applies to Christ (Rev.22:16), never to satan or earthly kings. Eliminating *Lucifer* allows the suggestion of Christ cast out of heaven instead of being sent by the Father as Savior of mankind. Thus a reader can imagine Christ blasphemed in referring to Himself as equal with God and was crucified and went to the grave as punishment. The Jehovah's Witnesses treat the passage rather similarly in the New World Version, but don't dare to use the title *morning star*.

Here the Hebrew can't be rendered *morning star* (or *day star*, 2 Pet.1:19). That title applies only to Christ the Creator who gave the light of life at the morning, or dawn, of creation (a true star is a light source). His divine glory was the light before creation of the sun (2 Cor.4:4-6). The KJB *Lucifer, son of the morning* (light-bearer) rightly signifies the archangel, a first-created son at creation morning. He was first to reflect light bestowed by Christ the Creator, and first to corrupt it (Venus, called the morning star, just reflects light of our sun, the true morning star, so Venus is a morning star). Differentiating terms for Christ and satan is vital, as seen by Rev.2:28 where believers receive the *morning star*, salvation in the person of Christ. This can't mean receiving Satan. Scripture doesn't assign or imply the title *morning star* or *day star* regarding Lucifer (or any earthly king).

In Job 38:7 the plural *morning stars* isn't a title, but a descriptive name for bright angels created at the beginning, as is plural *sons of God* in this verse. But the singular title *the morning star* or *the day star*, like the singular title *the son of God*, applies only to Christ, giver of light, not a created light-bearer at the morning of creation. In the Job verse, angels are stars in the sense of created bearers and reflectors of light, rather than sources of light.

The NIV *O morning star* is an address to an individual, and like *O son of God*, is more indicative of a title than a descriptive name. It can seem to refer to Christ in the NIV where there's a need to choose between Christ and lucifer as the morning star. With no lucifer there falling from heaven, Christ is the heavenly figure the title would likely refer to in this version. It was no earthly king of Babylon falling from heaven, for Christ says it was satan, or lucifer, and that's the only possible interpretation.

Use of *morning star* can't resemble a title to avoid confusing a reference to Christ with one to satan. The NASV avoids the main problem, inverting word order to lessen the sense of a title (*O star of the morning*). This suggests the angelic identity, for the figurative *star* can refer to angels. It's easily seen as figurative here, referring to a bright morning angel. The NASV committee was aware of the problem, but the NIV committee wasn't. The error is easily committed even by conscientious translators, but it's intolerable, confusing a reference to Christ with one to satan.

7. Providential Guidance: A Church in the Old Testament Era
Acts 7:38
This is he, (Moses) that was in the <u>church</u> in the wilderness with the angel which spake to him in the mount Sina...

KJB Providential guidance appears in use of the term *church* in Acts 7:38. Some think the KJB is anachronistic here in speaking of God's Old Testament wilderness wanderers under Moses as a *church in the wilderness*. They suppose the term *church* applies only to New Testament people who are recipients of the gospel, and are dependent on Christ for their needs and are under Christ's authority. But if we remember the definition of *church* and keep in mind the role of the preincarnate Christ in theophany in the lives of Old Testament people, we'll see there are times when it's proper to use the term *church* to refer to God's Old Testament people. What we'll see is an Old Testament typological church, even as we see types of Christ in the Old Testament.

The Greek for *church* in Acts 7:38 refers to a called-out gathering of people. When the term is used in reference to a church, it signifies a gathering of God's people called out of the world to be separate unto Him to follow Him, and that's what the wilderness wanderers were. God called them out of Egypt, that symbolizes the world, and they were gathered together and separated unto Him, following Him through the wilderness to Canaan.

The wilderness wanderers were a church in other senses of the word. They were a church in that the gospel was given to them. This is seen in Heb.4:2 that says, *For unto us was the gospel preached, as well as unto them* (wilderness wanderers – the gospel as defined by the rock and the brazen serpent noted below.

And they were a church in the sense that their needs were supplied by Christ. Paul informs us of this in telling us the water of life from the rock in the wilderness had a spiritual essence in that it was supplied by the preincarnate Christ who is the Rock of our faith (1 Cor.10:4, *And did all drink the same spiritual drink: for they drank of that spiritual Rock that followed them: and that Rock was Christ*). The wanderers are further shown to be a church with needs supplied by Christ in Heb.4:8 which speaks of Jesus as the one able to give them rest in the wilderness. And their need for sin-forgiveness was supplied by the brazen serpent that was lifted up and was typological of the Crucifixion.

Finally the wanderers were a church in that they were under Christ's authority. The logical reason Moses was not permitted to enter the promised land after striking the rock from which water came, would be that he struck that which symbolized Christ the authoritative head of the wilderness church. This is clear in an early account in Exo.17:1-7 with Moses commanded by God to strike the rock for water. This symbolizes smiting of Christ the suffering servant, the Rock of our faith, on the Cross so that the spiritual water of eternal life might come forth. Later, Numbers 20:1-13 shows Moses commanded by God to speak to the rock for water, which symbolizes asking the resurrected all-authoritative Christ for water of life (the gospel is presented). When Moses in anger with the people struck the rock the second time, this was a symbolic re-crucifixion of the all-authoritative resurrected head of the church. And when Moses referred to himself (and Aaron) as giving the water, he symbolically usurped Christ's role as the giver of water of eternal life. These are the likely reasons Moses was refused entrance to Canaan, the earthly promised land.

We further see Christ's authority over the wilderness wanderers in Joshua 5:13-15 that shows us Christ in theophany as *Captain of* the Host, before whom Joshua, the leader after Moses, bows before deciding Israel's actions in battle.

From our New Testament viewpoint, we see that the wilderness wanderers were a typological church in the wilderness, even though they didn't know it, and even though the term *church* was not then official. KJV translators were providentially guided to enlighten us over a matter we otherwise would not likely notice. Many moderns simply refuse the enlightenment.

And we should be able to see that the church instituted by God began typologically in an early primitive state and progressively developed throughout the Old Testament. We can see the church in existence in shadowy prefiguring forms from the beginning, for man's fall into sin was followed by a promise that the Savior, the head of the church, would bruise the head of the serpent satan in Genesis 3:15. And Abel's animal sacrifice for sin in Genesis 4:4 is logically a first response of man to God's requirement of an innocent offering for sin. Abel's offering prefigured animal sacrifice of the levitical system, which in turn prefigured the sacrifice of the perfect lamb of God on the Cross of Calvary.

A more developed church typology is seen in Noah and his family who, like the completed church, were called out to be separate from the world. They were placed in the ark of safety, and the ark was a prefigurer of Christ, the New Testament ark of safety. They, like the completed church, reside in God's ark of safety to spare them from God's judgment on the world.

The typological church was in a still more developed state at the time of the exodus when Christ in theophany directly controlled affairs of His called-out, separated Old Testament people.

All of this is in accord with Revelation 13:8 that tells us Christ, the king of the church, was God's plan from the beginning of mankind (the passage notes that Christ the Lamb was slain from the foundation of the world for mankind's salvation). The final step in the development of the church as God's institution was completed, and the church was openly and formally revealed to the world on the Day of Pentecost when God's Spirit was poured out upon men for empowerment of the church's work.

A Text Older than 4th-Century Alexandrian Manuscripts
The Traditional Text: Ancestor of the Received Text
1. Textual critic F.H.A. Scrivener placed the Italic in the 2nd century (*A Plain Introduction to N.T. Criticism*. Vol.2. p42-3). F. Kenyon, Alexandrian-text advocate, classified the Italic as of Traditional-Text type (*Our Bible and the Ancient Manuscripts*. Harper. p169-71).

2. The Gothic Bible is another text in the Traditional-Text mold.

The Traditional Text appears in the mid-4th century Gothic Bible of Teutonic peoples who invaded the Balkan Peninsula. A church was established among them in the mid-3rd century by Greek-speaking captive Christians of Asia Minor who had their Bible with them, and the Gothic translator was related to these Christians. Thus the Gothic New Testament was based on Traditional-Text Greek of the eastern Greek Church of Asia Minor, developed prior to the mid-3rd century. This refutes scholar theory on a mid-3rd to mid-4th century Traditional-Text invention. The apostle Paul ministered much in Asia Minor in the 1st century, and original Greek manuscripts would be placed there (Schaferdiek, K. 1991 *Christian Mission and Expansion*. "Early Christianity." ed I. Hazlett. Nashville. Abingdon Press. p65-76).

Italic and Gothic bibles are so alike they served as a bi-lingual for Romans and Goths, so they derived from the same type of Greek text (Hunter, M.J. 1969. *The Vernacular Scriptures: The Gothic Bible*. "*The Cambridge History of the Bible*. Cambridge Press. p338-60.

3. Egyptian 2nd-century papyri show Traditional-Text readings (Sturz, H.A. 1984. *The Byzantine Text Type and New Testament Textual Criticism*. Nelson. p55-76) along with Alexandrian ones,

indicating the Traditional circulated even in 2nd-century Egypt.

<u>4.</u> Egyptian papyri reveal Alexandrian readings derived from the Traditional, in keeping with Alexandrian text-corruption history.

Papyri indicate Byzantine (Traditional) readings trace deep into the 2nd century to refute Wescott & Hort who said the Byzantine was a 3rd-4th century invention derived by altering a supposedly original Alexandrian. Sturz notes an opposite trend, quoting writers who don't favor the Byzantine but admit that, in several cases, any tampering did not originate in the Byzantine. He quotes Tarelli who says a distinctive Byzantine John 11:19 reading is in a papyrus 100 years older than chief Alexandrian Vaticanus, and that any tampering is heaviest in the Alexandrian. He quotes Colwell who notes evidence in papyrus 66 that the Alexandrian scribe frequently changed Alpha (Traditional) readings to Beta (Alexandrian) ones. Sturz also says Byzantine scribes seem more conservative than Alexandrian ones in text preservation.

Sturz notes studies on papyrus P46 by Zuntz who finds the Byzantine Text, centered in Antioch, often unites with the Western text against the Alexandrian, united readings originating in the east. The two uniting texts developed separately, being widely separated geographically. The common readings indicate predominance of an eastern Byzantine text tracing at least as far back as deep in the 2nd century, spreading to the west and being copied there. Thus the Byzantine likely spread from east to west in early centuries since it paralleled spread of the church from east to west, as expected of an original apostolic text (it returned as the Received Text in the 16th century). This too refutes W & H theory of a Byzantine text derived from a supposedly more original Alexandrian. Sturz notes it's unlikely an older Antioch church, with its excellent scripture heritage, would early send to a younger Alexandrian church for manuscripts to correct its text (Sturz, Ibid). Indeed, conservative Antioch would never consult Alexandria known for its liberal spiritualizing of text interpretation.

<u>5.</u> The Syriac Peshitta version, of the Traditional-Text mold, was first categorized by scholars as of a 2nd century origin, but later was consigned to the 5th century by Westcott and Hort. It's origin is now seen as much earlier, in support of early scholarship.

Efforts to place the Peshitta origin in the 5th century AD, crediting it to Rabbula, bishop of Edessa, are now discredited. The two sects that the Syriac church divided into in the 5th century both adhered strictly to the Peshitta, and Rabbula led one of these sects. If the Peshitta were a 5th century invention of Rabbula, the other sect would never have accepted it as its authority. Clearly the Peshitta was the standard text of the Syriac church long before the 5th century so that Rabbula's use of it did not deter the other sect from using it. (Hills, E.F. *The King James Version Defended*. Christian Research Press. Des Moines. p172).

The Received Text and the KJB Preserve the Autographs

Greek Received-Text descent from the Traditional and a history of the Traditional tying it to the apostolic era, support the case for Received Text and KJB links to autographs. Proven passage authenticity, consistent accuracy, evidence of God's hand on the texts and a providentially-timed Received-Text advent indicate autograph-inerrancy preservation, so the Received Text corrects limited tampering in the Traditional to restore original inerrancy. Later dates of extant Traditional-Text copies just indicate the difficulty in preserving much-used fragile copies, and their 94% majority in extant manuscripts offers significance of consistency.

Scholars still say 4th-century Alexandrian manuscripts have the oldest and best extant texts, despite many doctrinal/textual flaws, and they still discredit the Received text and KJB. But the best evidence is traceable text history, usage in true churches being a hallmark of God's Word, for that's where the text is most needed and valued. Elsewhere, manuscripts fall prey to meddlers or indifferent scholars.

Summarized Conclusions from the Evidence Presented.

1. Consistent incomparable accuracy, generally misjudged by agenda-driven modern scholars, humbles their modern texts.

2. Passages scorned by scholars prove to be authentic, the 1 Jn.5: 7,8 Johannine Comma and the case of Jonah and the big fish being especially-informative examples of proven authenticity.

3. Evidence of text divine inspiration and guidance, account for inerrancy indicated by consistent accuracy and authenticity.

4. Eternal word preservation is a proven promise of scripture.

5. The advent of the Greek Received Text was providentially-timed, being enabled and upheld by major historical events.

6. The Traditional-Text ancestor of the Greek Received Text can be traced at least as far back as the 2nd century A.D. and the Hebrew Masoretic Text at least as far as the 5th-4th centuries B.C.

7. Authenticity, accuracy and history indicate the Greek Received Text corrects limited error imposed on Traditional-Text manuscripts located outside biblical churches over the centuries to restore autograph inerrancy. Regarding the Masoretic Text, this writer's studies continually indicate sustained inerrancy.

A Final Note

The reader can plainly see that scholars only mar our view of the text that God has given to guide us through the difficulties and hazards of the earthly life. Our confidence must rest in God alone to preserve His Word for us and ensure that we know the truth. Text history indicates that He has always done so for His people, as the reader can further see from Appendix A below.

Epilogue
Preservation of Inerrancy and the State of the Bible Text in Extant Manuscripts

Comments of scholars today on text quality, based on variance in extant Greek manuscripts, confuse laymen regarding inerrancy and the reliability of the Bible. But scholars seem unaware that extant manuscripts reveal a preservation reflecting the measure of faith among Bible-believers, in contrast with a lack of faith among others. That is to say, we might expect God to preserve the word in its inerrant original state for true Bible-believers who desire to follow Him to the fullest extent, while providing enough truth to unbelievers to allow them to come to a state of true faith. Thus the state of the text would reflect God's guidance of people and nations on the basis of the desire to know the wisdom of His truth so that each person is made responsible for His own attitude and thus can be fairly and rightly subjected to final judgment.

Thus it is no surprise that the Hebrew Masoretic Text of a God-conscious people, who emphasized scripture's inviolable nature in Old-Testament days (though they didn't always obey it), has been preserved without significant manuscript variance (contrary to scholar opinion, and illustrated in this writer's books). In those days the way to God was to join the Hebrew nation, so the text applied to Hebrews and Gentiles who recognized their God, and there was no known book of revelation from the true God for those remaining outside the nation.

With Greek manuscripts the situation is complex, but predictable, being based on the church as God's instrument for people to come to a state of true faith. Some major Bible passages, such as those on the Johannine Comma, with its crucial support of Trintarian doctrine and the eunuch's confession of Jesus as the Son of God, would be preserved in an inerrant state in the relatively few extant manuscripts linked to historical small biblical churches of the medieval era, while a lack of these truths would exist in manuscripts located in historical large unbiblical churches of that era. And in modern times, marked by rampant heathenism and carnality that have invaded many churches, the worst possible manuscripts, those of the Alexandrian text, are the ones applied to translations of most churches. Further, the best of all extant manuscripts, those of the Traditional Text that present consistent soundness and date to the 10th-11th centuries in the majority of cases, would reflect resurgence of truth for translation in an Italic Latin text of biblical churches that originated in apostolic days and received new prominence through the Waldenses' influence throughout Europe beginning in the 12th century. Finally, the Received Text, printed in the 16th century shortly before the Reformation, marked a return from religious tradition to biblical faith. The Received Text became the foundation for Separatist and biblical Baptist churches in England, and it would constitute a restored inerrant Traditional Text, especially needed today since the end of the church era and the end of all opportunity to follow God by His Word is evidently approaching.

Summarizing the matter, general error in extant Greek manuscripts would reflect the historic error of "churches" that ignore God and scorn the Traditional Text, and a preference for critical-text versions today would signify satisfaction with the error in "churches" given over to error of all kinds, while an inerrant text would guide God's scattered faithful churches in true translations.

The KJV represents British and American history characterized by widespread sound biblical Christian faith, in contrast with a scattered minority in churches today that hold to this faith, while others widely adopt translations of Greek critical texts. Further, the KJV marks the greatest epochs of English-language history, appearing shortly before the successful establishment of the Plymouth colony in America in 1620, and it shortly followed the colonists to become the Bible of America. It was foundational to American epochs like the Great Awakening in New England and the greatest Bible-based missionary work since the apostolic era. In England the KJV was the standard that guided the writing of Pilgrim's Progress by John Bunyan. It was the Bible of the great revivals that so notably affected Britain and America in the early 18th century and afterwards. It was the Bible of great missionary work of William Carey in India in the 18th-19th centuries, during which he translated scripture into 40 other languages. The KJV accompanied 19th century spread of British empire over the world from Europe and the Americas to Asia, Australia and Africa, so it's a world-wide vehicle of God's Word. The KJV encompasses a history of God's plan that would require standards of accuracy indicative of preserved inerrancy, for it's been used and blessed of God in unusual ways that speak of His sovereign ordination.

All this is a logical position for all who trust in the sovereignty of God over His creation. It is far more logical for true Christians to believe in God's sovereign control of His Word than it is to rely on opinions of mere men, scholars who are part of the creation, and must yield to the Creator Himself.

Some inane modern-day objections to KJV inerrancy
We conclude with comment on a few objections to inerrancy of the KJV that further demonstrate the irrelevance of objections.

1. Some commentators emphasize printing error, as if that denied text inerrancy. An inerrant text is preserved, but no one claims inerrancy for every copy of the text, and correction of printing error is part of the process of imparting inerrancy to copies in general. Language/grammar up-dating that has occurred in KJV history seems to some to deny KJV inerrancy, but such up-dating is needed at times to ensure communication of inerrant scriptural teaching to readers in general.

2. Some internet commentators argue that scripture itself doesn't say the KJV is God's Word. Well it also doesn't say any certain Greek and Hebrew/Aramaic texts are God's Word. Obviously scripture won't say such things, for that would remove freedom of choice and make English-speaking people use only the KJV and its textual basis. People have a right to choose inventions of men, in preference to God's Word if they wish to, just as they have the right to choose salvation-by-works philosophy of men, in preference to God's salvation by grace that scripture teaches. They're permitted to prefer evolutionism insanity over teaching of creation in God's Word if they prefer to live like animals. They're permitted to rationalize away the natural disasters and economic hardships that befall a nation that turns its back on God, their views allowing them to retain their carnal liberal life-styles. We're all given the right of choice in all things so that we might be fairly and rightly judged in the day of final judgment.

3. Some internet commentators make the silly point that KJV translators never claimed their text was inerrant. Well, translators making that claim would reveal a gigantic egoism that would disgust serious readers. The modesty of KJV translators in regard to their work, despite their unparalleled scholarship, is indicative of reverence for God and His Word. God doesn't honor arrogant men, but chooses the humble and reverent, and in the case of the KJV committee, He chose men who also had scholarship credentials far beyond those of scholars today. But today we encounter some scholars who think they are the means by which God's Word is preserved. They suggest God's true Word is scattered among manuscripts so that they must identify it, separating it from that which is corrupted. One result is that long-lost Greek Alexandrian manuscripts, filled with much error, are artificially made a standard of preference. Another result, promotion of texts of manuscripts lost to churches for 1400-1500 years, suggests God wasn't able to preserve His Word for His people over those centuries, and had to wait for modern scholars to accomplish this.

Appendix A

God's Word in the Life of His People: The Available History

Introduction

Biblical Christianity is totally misrepresented today, especially the present writer's Biblical Fundamentalism that seeks to preserve traditional biblical truth, for which scholars attack us. Newsmen link the name to jihad fanatics that kill innocent people. Liberal commentators label us as intolerant for warning people of the dangers of immorality and man-made religion, as if warnings against self-destruction were somehow wrong. Compromising clergy accuse us of being too narrow and too intent on orthodoxy just because we desire a pure biblical faith, with God's Word, not men's opinion, guiding our lives and destiny. And some claiming to be biblical fundamentalists don't live up to the name.

Preserving biblical truth is never easy, and promoting it is always widely unpopular due to man's sin nature, and many prefer their own version of truth. At times the light of biblical truth has been obscured or eclipsed by unholy religious/political forces that have tried to eliminate it throughout the nearly 2000 years of the church era. In more recent times, problems have been caused mainly by irreverent humanism that, in various unholy forms, has spawned a modernism rampage that greatly threatens all truly conservative churches.

The True Church Unchanging

The state of churches is generally poor in modern times, but there is still a remnant following the truth, as has always been the case. A company of true Christians has upheld biblical truth from the beginning of the church era. Skeptical scholars, our worst problem, reject such claims, saying all biblical conservatives, including Baptist fundamentalists, originated in the 16th century Protestant Reformation. Those denying origination of the biblical churches in the apostolic era place the earliest one in the 12th century one called Waldensen after Peter Waldo. But such opinion just parrots a popular widely published historical record made by those who oppose biblical belief. The Waldenses, a true biblical church with roots in an apostolic-era church, came to be known by this name as a result of the work of Peter Waldo in the 12th century (The Roman church applied this name to them, and is it any wonder that they, who claim apostolic succession for themselves, would try to limit the Waldenses to late history?) As for the notion that biblical churches originated in the 16th century Reformation, churches originating in that movement never were fully biblical, never breaking fully with non-biblical Roman tradition that they sprang from. Yet the Reformation later produced churches that follow biblical faith in a strict conservative fashion.

Christ's Testimony: All denial of an apostolic-era origin of the true church of today is refuted by Christ, the divine founder and power of the church who has always energized upholding of biblical truth. In Mt.16:18 He said, *I will build my church; and the gates of hell shall not prevail against it*. Christ's words can have a dual sense, and in one sense, *gates of hell* signify the entrance to hell opened up to unwise souls by unbiblical religion and political powers that try to force people to abandon Christ's truth of the Bible. They use persecution in trying to open the gates of hell to the church Christ builds, but the gates can't prevail against souls belonging to Christ, or can't open and imprison the souls of those who trust in Christ by His Word. And gates of hell, passageways through which hell's powers in the form of false religion and political forces are released on earth, can't prevail against and defeat the church Christ builds and preserves in its work of winning souls to the truth of His Word.

But if we believe modern scholars, we'll think Christ's promise to uphold the church founded on His Word failed early in history. The church in the New Testament is very different from non-biblical western Roman and eastern Greek churches that dominated the medieval era. If no biblical church endured in this period, and beyond, that would mean Christ's church was defeated. It would mean the gates of hell did prevail over the biblical church, from a time before the 5th century, up to and beyond the biblical awakening of the 16th-century Reformation.

But Christ is God and Creator, and He informs us that a church founded upon His Word persisted throughout the church era, so true conservatives look for evidence of an historical church fulfilling His Matthew 16 words. It will accord well with the New Testament description of the church and will have an origin tracing back to very early history. Baptist Fundamentalist churches fulfill these criteria as New Testament churches fully identified with biblical belief from the earliest church history.

A true-church history: History refutes modern opinion on the origin of Baptists with evidence that fundamentalist belief has an ancient origin. But knowledge of doctrine and practice of early Bible-based groups is complicated since reports by their enemies are the main available accounts. Their beliefs would be distorted by their enemies, and several were called heretical just because they disagreed with the popular non-biblical religion of their day. Writings of these groups would be systematically destroyed, and their self-views would never be included in popular writings of their day (today fundamentalists are slandered without much recourse, their views being ignored by the popular publishers). Today scholars take the easy route on the history of these groups, accepting comments on their beliefs made by their enemies, so conclusions on the groups in modern publications lack validity. Indeed pertinent research shows that groups labeled as heretical for resisting popular non-biblical religion of their day had beliefs in common with fundamentalists today. This is true especially regarding doctrines of the supremacy of the Bible as God's Word, a regenerate church membership, believer's baptism and church independence of hierarchy and all external authority of an ecclesiastical nature.

Groups with fundamentalist Baptist-like beliefs appear early in history. Strict Baptist conservatives most recently follow pre-Reformation Anabaptists (re-baptizers), who follow Waldenses of earlier origin, who in turn follow the Vaudois of still-earlier origin. The Waldensen name derives from a 12th-century leader, but their faith traces to the 2nd century through their Italic Bible derived from Vaudois ancestors, as we'll see. Waldenses and their Vaudois ancestors were centered in northern Italy and southern France, and influenced many in their locale and beyond.

Scriptural doctrines held by Baptists have influenced many throughout the centuries, and we can trace that influence. With regard to Anabaptists, contrary to published reports, 16th-century notables didn't start this movement, but joined it after departing from original Reformation churches that didn't become fully biblical. Anabaptists took different paths from the Reformation that clouded their origin at times, but some kept to a Baptist-like faith that had influenced many throughout the centuries. Pre-Reformation Baptist doctrines like those of Anabaptists are seen in the *United Brethren* at Prague. These arose from 15th-century teachings of former Catholic-priest John Hus, whose teachings in turn trace back to John Wycliffe in England in the 14th century. Baptist doctrines are seen in notable groups that broke with the Roman church in the 12th century, like the Petrobrusians led by Peter of Bruys in France, Henricians led by Henry of Lausanne in France and Arnoldists led by Arnold of Bresica in Italy. And in the 3rd-9th centuries, Celtic Christians with Baptist-type beliefs constituted Christianity in the British Isles. And historical literature offers some information on independent groups like Donatists, Novations and Montanists, who had variant degrees of orthodoxy, but were all influenced to some degree by doctrines today identified with Baptists. The Donatists of North Africa in the 4th-7th centuries seem very orthodox, emphasizing authority of the Bible in the churches, church independence and the church as a visible elect body pure from carnality. The Montanists and

Novatians, originating in the 2nd and 3rd centuries respectively, emphasized authority of scripture, independence of churches and purity of living. In all such historic groups, biblical influence can stem ultimately only from the initial 1st-century standard biblical church founded by Christ.

Further history on Baptist-like groups further illustrates their independence and their origin in ancient times.

(a) H.C. Vedder, *A Short History of the Baptists*, p128-30."And it is a curious and instructive fact that the Anabaptist churches of the Reformation period were most numerous precisely where the Waldenses of a century or two previous had most flourished, and where their identity as Waldenses had been lost....Those who maintain that the Anabaptists originated with the Reformation have some difficult problems to solve, among others the rapidity with which the leaven spread, and the wide territory that the Anabaptists so soon covered. Another problem demanding solution is furnished by the fact that these Anabaptist churches were not gradually developed, but appear fully formed from the first – complete in polity, sound in doctrine, strict in discipline. It will be found impossible to account for these phenomena without an assumption of a long-existing cause."

(b) E.H. Broadbent, *The Pilgrim Church*, p89,90. "In the Alpine valleys of Piedmont there had been for centuries congregations of believers calling themselves brethren, who came later to be widely known as Waldenses, or Vaudois, though they did not themselves accept the name…these were not "reformed" never having degenerated from the New Testament pattern as had the Roman, Greek and some others, but having always maintained, in varying degrees, the apostolic tradition."

(c) L.P. Brockett, *The Bogomils of Bulgaria and Bosnia*, 11,12. "…I have found often in unexpected quarters, the most conclusive evidence that these sects were all, during their earthly history, Baptists, not only in their views on the subjects of baptism and the Lord's Supper, but in their opposition to Paedobaptism (infant baptism), to a church hierarchy, and to the worship of the virgin Mary and the saints, and in their adherence to church independency and freedom of conscience in religious worship. In short, the conclusion has forced itself upon me that in these Christians of Bosnia, Bulgaria and Armenia we have an apostolic succession of Christian churches, New Testament churches…"

(d) J.T. Christian in Baptist magazine CVIII, 278. May, 1826, quotes one cardinal Hosius, who, at the 1524 A.D. Council of Trent, spoke candidly, placing persecution of Anabaptists as early as the 4th century. In *Hosius, Letters, Apud Opera*, p112,113 we read, "If the truth of religion were to be judged by the readiness and boldness of which a man of any sect shows in suffering, then the opinion and persuasion of no sect can be truer and surer than that of the Anabaptists since there have been none for these twelve hundred years past that have been more generally punished or that have more cheerfully and steadfastly undergone, and even offered themselves to the most cruel sorts of punishment than these people." [1]

(e) Robert Olivetan, the Waldensen scholar responsible for the 1535 A.D. French Bible that bears his name, wrote in the preface, "Since the time of the apostles, or their immediate successors, the torch of the gospel has been lit among the vaudois, and has never since been extinguished."

(f) Par Jean Leger in his, *General History of the Evangelical Churches in the Piedmontese Valleys*, 1669 A.D, wrote concerning the confession of faith of these churches, "This confession is that, which we have received from our ancestors, even from hand to hand, according to their predecessors, in all times and in every age, have taught and delivered."

(g) J.A. Wylie, a Presbyterian historian in his, *History of Waldenses*, 1860 A.D, wrote, "Their traditions invariably point to an unbroken descent from earliest times, as regards their religious belief. The *Noble Lesson*, that dates from the year 1100 A.D., goes to prove that the Waldenses of Piedmont did not owe their rise to Peter Waldo of Lyons, who did not appear until the latter half of that century (1160). The *Noble Lesson*, though a poem, is in reality a confession of faith, and could have been composed only after some considerable study of the system of Christianity, in contradistinction to the errors of Rome."

As for doctrine, Rome persecuted them due to great differences of their biblical doctrine with the unbiblical Roman-church type.

(a) One Reinerius Saccho of the 13th century lived with the Waldenses for 17 years and later persecuted them. He wrote the pope about Waldensen doctrine in 1250, saying, "They rejected the Roman church, believing it to be the whore of Babylon. They claimed that Rome erred in yoking with

1. It's interesting that a Roman-church adversary can relate the Anabaptist name to very early history, while "neutral' modern scholars can't.

the secular government in the days of Constantine. They rejected the mass and claimed that the bread is only symbolic. They rejected infant baptism because babies cannot believe. They rejected the Catholic priests and bishops. They rejected extreme unction, saying it is a curse rather than a sacrament. They rejected purgatory, believing that the dead go either to heaven or hell. They rejected prayers to the dead. They did not believe in the prayers of the saints. They rejected confession of sins to a priest, believing that sins should be confessed only to God

(b) John Wesley wrote, "And it was given him (the antichrist) – That is God permitted him to make war with his saints – With the Waldenses and Albigenses. It is a vulgar mistake, that the Waldenses were so called from Peter Waldo of Lyons. They were much more ancient than him; and their true name was Vallenses or vaudois from their inhabiting the valleys of Lucerne and Agrogne. This name, Vallenses, after Waldo appeared about the year 1160, was changed by the papists into Waldenses, on purpose to represent them as of modern original. The Albigenses were originally people of Albigeois, part of Upper Languedoc, where they considerably prevailed and possessed several towns in the year 1200. Against these many of the popes made open war. Till now the blood of Christians had been shed only by the heathens or Arians; from this time by scarce any but the papacy. In the year 1208 Innocent III proclaimed a crusade against them. In June, 1209, the army assembled at Toulouse, from which time abundance of blood was shed, and the second army of martyrs began to be added to the first, who had cried "from beneath the altar." And ever since, the beast has been warring against the saints, and shedding their blood like water. And authority was given him over every tribe and people – particularly in Europe. And when a way was found by sea into the East Indies, and the West, these also were brought under his authority.

There were doctrinal differences among historic biblical groups, as there are today among true conservatives, for the liberty of true faith allows secondary differences. Some groups broke with Roman and Greek churches to adopt freedom of conscience of Baptist-type beliefs. There were even some that mixed Baptist belief with ancient heresy, indicating they were exposed to the gospel light. But throughout the history of religion in a world darkened by satan, Christ has preserved His true church, and it has always had basic biblical faith, despite political dominance and cruel persecution by non-biblical religion, and despite confusion of heresy. That the true church was a small minority, while non-biblical and mixed religion were a large majority, is no surprise. Christ said in Matthew 7:13,14... *wide is the gate, and broad is the way, that leadeth to destruction, and many there be which go in thereat: Because strait is the gate, and narrow is the way, which leadeth unto life, and few there be that find it.*

Many scholars believe Baptists originated in the Reformation left wing in England, but this is assumption that can't be shown to be true to scripture or history. True Baptist churches, being distinct from those originating in the 16th century Reformation, have one possible origin, the New Testament church founded by Christ. The Reformation "left wing" was just a later dissatisfied group of reformers that held some Baptist concepts and adopted various left-wing concepts in their quest to be different from earlier reformers. Mixing of truth and error has always been popular with much of mankind, for men who follow their sin nature have always wanted something of both earth and heaven.

Now publicized Baptist-church history began in England in ~1611 (in close association with publication of our KJB), but that was just the first public recognition in Europe. Groups with biblical Baptist-like beliefs had for many centuries suffered great persecution that made sustained organized work impossible and kept them in the shadows of history. They had endured a long history of persecution by Rome, and more lately by Henry VIII, Mary Tudor and Elizabeth I. But their cause gained vigor in the early 17th century since Church-of-England Puritans, seeking reformation of their state church, had recently been promoting Baptist concepts. The influence of bible-oriented Puritans was strong in the reign of Elizabeth and in the 1603-1625 reign of James I, and their reform effort was aided by circulation of the Geneva Bible (reflecting the Tyndale) that increased public awareness of scripture. As Puritans pursued reform, their views developed along biblical lines, leading to formation of Baptist-like separatists. Eventually some groups naturally adopted much existing biblical Baptist-like belief, leading them to establish churches called Baptist to distinguish them from less-biblical ones. The Baptist name derived from biblical Anabaptists of earlier history, and biblical theology of Anabaptists and their ancestors was adopted, so only the name was new. The Puritan movement was prominent, and the impetus it gave to biblical Anabaptist faith gave a new name to, and brought into written history, Baptist-like churches previously suppressed and forced underground for many centuries. Thus centuries of repression of the writings of Anabaptists and their ancestors on the struggle for liberty finally came to a halt. This is the logical reason why the widely-known Baptist writings begin in the early 17th century, and is the reason they dwell so much on non-biblical religion, freedom of religion and separation of church and state.

This history is like a sawdust trail that begins at a sawmill. If wind removes all of the trail but a final short distance sheltered by trees, did the trail not originate at the sawmill? This portrays Baptist history, but the "wind" of persecution didn't remove all traces of the origin. Research has revealed evidences of Baptist doctrines in groups whose origin is in the ancient past so that fundamentalists and all true conservatives can see them as upholding the New Testament faith we love so dearly.

The True Text of God's True People

A people whose struggle for liberty in faith originates in the apostolic era, have always had a biblical standard, which relates to why strict conservatives adhere fully to the King James Bible (the Authorized Version). The KJB Greek Received Text derives from the Traditional Text tracing to the Bible of our spiritual forebears, Waldenses and their Vaudois ancestors centered in northern Italy and southern France, who trace their history to the apostolic era. They endured efforts of Rome to destroy them and their Bible. That Bible, their strength in the face of persecution, had a New Testament that was an apostolic-era original.

The Greek Received Text of the KJV New Testament is represented very early in church history in the traditional-type text of the Italic Old Latin Bible of the Vaudois/Waldensen church. This is seen despite Jerome's textual meddling that altered the state of the early Latin text. The Italic was the basis for Jerome's Vulgate New Testament,[2,3] as well as the Vaudois/Waldensen Bible, but he imposed another Greek text, the Alexandrian, at places in his Vulgate. And he may have altered an Italic to make it agree with the Alexandrian (Nolan notes a dissimilarity once existing between the old Italic and the Vulgate and Greek of the Alexandrian text, but changed in the Italic of Jerome's day [3]). The Italic Traditional-Text nature is verified by Warner who says,[4] *The version current among the western heretics* (Waldenses, biblical churches called heretics by Catholics) *can be shown to be based upon the Greek* (Traditional Text) *and not the Latin* (Vulgate) And 17th-century scholar Allix said of Waldensen worship,[5] *The liturgy* (his vernacular) *has the Psalms and diverse other texts of Scripture of the ancient version called the Italic.* Extant Tepl and Romaunt Waldensen Bible versions reflect the Vulgate in general due to a common Italic basis, but they agree against the Vulgate at places,[6] suggesting the versions follow the Traditional Text where Jerome imposed the Alexandrian. In the 16th century Beza called Waldensen ancestors, the Vaudois, *the*

2. Rypins, S. 1951. *The Book of Thirty Centuries*. MacMillan. p168.
3. Nolan, F. *An Inquiry into the Integrity of the Greek Vulgate or Received Text of the New Testament*. R. & R. Gilbert. St. John's Sq. Clerkenwell,England. Ch.1
4. Warner, J.H. 1922-28. Soc. for Promotion of Christian Knowledge MacMillan.
5. Allix, P, D.D. *Remarks upon the Ecclesiastical History of the Ancient Churches of the Albigenses*. Ch.7, p51. 1989 ed. Reprint from 1821 ed.
6.Hurst, J.F. 1897.*History of the Christian Church*, Vol.1. Eaton/Mains. NY. p834.

most pure primitive Christian church. Waldensen pastor Leger in the 17th century said Waldenses originated in apostolic times.[7] This church would retain an apostolic scripture text, explaining why they didn't vary from basic biblical orthodoxy until after the Reformation. Leger said they, *always had the entire joy and fruition of the celestial treasure of the true preserved holy scripture,*[7] and this is verified in their rejection of the Latin Vulgate with its Alexandrian-Text influence.

Thus the Received Text of our KJV New Testament derives from a text our spiritual forebears held to in resisting persecution by Rome. Jerome corrupted the Italic text, using it as a basis and adding error of the Alexandrian text from dark Egypt and the unorthodox theologian Origen to produce the Roman Vulgate. Modern bible versions champion Alexandrian-text error, and we today will no more accept this than did our spiritual ancestors.

More Historic Testimonies on the True Text

(a) The great textual scholar of the 19th century, F.H.A. Scrivener, placed the origin of the Old Latin Bible, of which the Italic was the most reliable, as a translation from the Greek at ~150 A.D.

(b) The great historian Frederick Nolan spent 28 years studying the history of the Italic version, and in 1815 said, "A very short process enables us to prove that the tradition which supports the authority of this text has continued unbroken since the age of the apostles. The coincidence of the Vulgar Greek of our present editions (Received Text) with the old Italic translation, enables us to carry up the tradition to the times of (St.) Jerome. The particular manner in which the western church delivers its testimony, in confirmation of that of the Greek church, seems almost decisive in evincing the permanence and purity of the text of Byzantium (Traditional Text). The Brescia manuscript, which contains this testimony, possesses a text which, as composed of the Old Italic version, must be antedated to the year 393, when the new version was made by (St.) Jerome.

7. Sorenson, D.H. 2001. *Touch not the Unclean Thing*. Northstar. p256-61.

(c) Emilio Comba in his 1889, *History of the Waldenses of Italy: from their origin to the Reformation*, said the Tepl Bible used by Luther in his translation work was a Waldensen translation. He states that the Tepl was based on Old Latin manuscripts rather than Jerome's Latin Vulgate.

(d) J.T Christian in his *The history of Baptists*, says, "There had been more than one translation of the Bible into German before Luther's time. The Baptists used with great power their heritage of the Waldensen Bible, and they hailed with delight Luther's translation of the Bible."

Concluding Statement

Today scholars reject our King James Bible in favor of modern versions based on a critical-type text that, in turn is based almost entirely on the Alexandrian Text, the type that displays much doctrinal and textual inaccuracy. They abandon the old ways, opting for supposedly superior scholarship of today. They often demean the KJB and those who defend it. They're in a company that advocate the widely-published record of the history of the true conservative church as originating with the Reformation or Peter Waldo. They disdain the record of continuity of the true biblical church from the apostolic era, and so they disdain the words of the Christ who promised to sustain it.

The reader has seen testimony by those who proclaim that the true church extends in a line of descent tracing to the apostolic era. They believed Christ's Word, and sympathized with biblical churches in their persecution at the hand of false religionists, and their convictions conflict with the claims of modern scholars who show so little concern for truth. So who will the reader believe, Christ and His faithful people or the modern advocates of man's scholarship? To give the reader more insight into errors of modern scholarship, some modern views of the scripture text are presented in the addendum below.

*Some other sources referenced by the writer: J.M. Carroll. *The Trail of Blood*. Byron Page Printing Co. Lexington, KY and Kentbrandenburg-blogspot.com "What is Truth: The Waldenses Controversy.'

Addendum to Appendix A

Readers can get a further idea of the erroneous aspects of methods of modern scholarship by considering the higher-criticism tenets.

Higher criticism "criticized"

Source criticism: This seeks to identify human literary sources and precursors behind a scripture text,[1] in an effort to reduce scripture to a faulty history book. It arose from observations like the fact that in the Pentateuch Moses is at times spoken of in the 3rd person in a statement like, *The Lord spake unto Moses.* Scholars suggest this indicates a later writer recorded his private views of what transpired in Moses' life. But Moses likely wrote parts of the books personally and dictated parts to an associate so that the authorship was always that of Moses, while the writing itself was often that of the associate, as was the case with Paul's epistles. Actually common use of the 3rd person in the Pentateuch shows that the writer doesn't dare to misrepresent matters, as expected of one dealing with sacred truth.

But the scripture message requires more of the associate than taking dictation. He had to record Moses' death, and he wrote other items that Moses couldn't write or dictate, such as...*Moses was very meek, above all the men which were upon the face of the earth* (Num.12:3). The Spirit dictates to Moses, but a close associate recording Moses' words for inscripturation is ordained of God as an extension of the prophet's voice, sharing in the Spirit's direction of the prophet in adding error-free notes. This process reflects the gospel by Mark, who wasn't an apostle, but was an associate of the apostle and scripture-penman, Peter, their association and Mark's sharing in the Spirit's leading of Peter being a likely basis for Mark's gospel (Mark's writing was even said to interpret Peter).

1. Johnson, R. 1996. *Modern Old Testament Interpretation.* Biblical Hermeneutics. Nashville. Broadman. p101-8.

Now it's possible some scripture penmen used written sources. But this writer contends that, in such cases these wouldn't be just man's accounts of his society, but divinely <u>authorized select</u> parts of written tradition fully consistent with verbal/plenary inspiration. This would be a kind of divine dictation in the form of writing, comparable to the case of Exodus 34:1 where God gave Moses scripture in His divine writing on stone tables. Further, sources can apply if one scripture book references others, as in the case of Chronicles that references Samuel/Kings revelation in order to amplify or expound the text

Another possible case of source usage is the Genesis account by Moses who may have used records on the history of Adam in Eden in the first few chapters. Contrary to scholars, language originated with Adam since he spoke with God and his family and named animals. He may have had writing ability by creation, and it's possible he wrote an account of his times preserved in copies in certain languages. If Moses used such an account, the proper parts would be authorized by God for inclusion in the Pentateuch in Moses' communion with God during the exodus. But it's far more likely that God gave Moses the necessary account verbally, as was the case with the law on Sinai.

And other documents may have been authorized sources for parts of scripture. Scholars say scripture indicates this from various verses like Joshua 10:13 and Numbers 21:14. But use of sources isn't at all certain in such verses. Joshua 10:13, that's illustrative of passages of this type, says, *And the sun stood still, and the moon stayed, until the people had avenged themselves upon their enemies. Is not this written in the <u>book of Jasher</u>?* There's no justification to interpret this as noting anything more than recording of details of the event in non-canonical Jasher, as well as canonical Joshua. The book of Jasher is likely noted as a second source of fact since the event is so unique. There's no reason to exclude from scripture accurate historical references, and it's to be expected that secular accounts will be written on such unique events, along with related matters. Skeptics make too much of the idea of sources, and in the process would reduce scripture authority to that of a fallible history book. Select parts of providentially-authorized non-canonical written sources may have been used, but more likely they are quoted as a second source of fact regarding an event (the book of Joshua won't say, Is not this recorded in this book of Joshua?)

The documentary hypothesis; This denies Mosaic authorship of the Pentateuch, attributing it to four sources living centuries after Moses. It suggests Pentateuch credibility on history is minimal and patriarchal history is man's invention. But studies show it was based on poor scholarship that misrepresents scripture. It was highly regarded for a long time, but its error was exposed by archaeological studies that agree with Pentateuch historical data on customs, names, laws, etc. for the proper times in history. The facts support Mosaic authorship and chronology and refute the theory. Indeed writers in late times postulated in the theory couldn't possibly have the close familiarity with early data seen in the Pentateuch and verified by archaeology.[2]

Interpretation error: Superficial scholarship underlying source criticism and resultant error are glaringly obvious in the proposal that chapters one and two of Genesis derive from two different sources with two different discordant accounts of the creation. Common sense tells us chapter one gives a broad treatment of the creation, and chapter two, gives a closer more specific view of the creation concentrating on Adam and his near environment, which is a common type of literary device.

2. Archeological studies often uncover documents with names of cities, persons and business of society recorded in the Pentateuch. - See Davis Dictionary of the Bible. 1973. Nashville. Royal. p621.
-See also Thompson, J.A. 1962. *The Bible and Archaeology*. Gr.Rapids
-Eerdemans. p70, 71.
-See also McDowell, J. 1979. *Evidence that Demands a Verdict*. Vol.1. Nashville. Nelson. p68-70.

Superficial scholarship underlying source criticism includes a supposition of discordant double references to a specific incident in scripture that suggests to scholars different discordant sources of the text. Examples offered include supposed twice naming of Bethel by Jacob (Gen.28:19 & 35:15) and changing of Jacob's name to Israel twice (Gen. 32:28 & 35:10). But these are not discordant double references to certain events, but accounts of similar matters in related, but different, circumstances.

In Genesis 28:19 Jacob fleeing from Esau rests in a place where he encounters God. The text says, *he called the name of that place Bethel: but the name of that city was called Luz at the first*, contrasting two names for one city at the same time. In 35: 15, years later, he's again in distress, over a different matter, some killings by his sons, and he returns to Bethel, seeking renewal of God's guidance. In both Genesis verses, the town is called Luz by locals, and 35:6 says, *Luz...that is Bethel*, again relating two names for one city at the same time. In 35:15 Jacob didn't name the town a first time but returned, reaffirming his preferred name for the place, one that hadn't taken hold at that time, but would one day. Bethel means "House of God" and that's what it was to Jacob since he met God there. But it was still Luz to the locals, and Jacob's preference likely motivated a later name change. We too have "back to Bethel" experiences in times of trouble when we return to our Bethel in an effort to find our way, and we reaffirm our commitment to God.

In Genesis 32:28 Jacob wrestles with an angel of God who tells him he has power with God and that his, *name shall be called no more Jacob, but Israel...*which speaks of a promise to come. The later fulfillment of the promise is seen in Genesis 35:10 which says, *Thy name is Jacob* (It was still Jacob at that point but is about to be changed to fulfill the earlier promise) *thy name shall not be called any more Jacob* (This is God's ending of that name for him), *but Israel shall be thy name: and he called his name Israel* (the change occurred just once, at this time).

The so-called Synoptic Problem: New Testament source criticism addresses causes for similarities and differences among the
three synoptic gospels.[3] Critics note concerning Mark's shorter
gospel that much of it is very similar to Luke's and Matthew's
gospels, so they suppose naturalistic causes. They suggest that
Mark's gospel was written first and Luke and Matthew copied
from him, adding things. Or they suggest Matthew was first and
was used by Luke, both being edited by Mark. Thus they don't
know which gospel was first, or who used what, and they're just
speculating. They see incidents in Luke and Matthew that, together, or separately, aren't in Mark, so they invent other sources,
one of which the two writers had in common. Sources are the
only possible basis for the gospels according to these critics.

There is remarkable similarity among the synoptics that includes much verbatim wording and a similar non-chronological
order of events that are unexpected of independent writers. But
remarkable agreement in the gospels illustrates a common guide,
God, controlling different writers, and differences in detail
illustrate the independent status of writers God controls. Much
overall and specific agreement, along with aspects confined to
one or two gospels, shows that writers giving the same message
from God are independent authors. Mark's shorter gospel shows
his status as an independent writer of common scriptural events,
and further details by Matthew and Luke complete the common
message and show their independent status. We consider a prominent pertinent example, the Christmas story. Luke's unique
details show his independent status, and differences in Matthew
complete the common message and point up his status as an
independent writer of God's message. As we'll see, while the
penmen are allowed variance in expression, the differences fit
perfectly into the overall account. Thus the fact of four gospels
with parallel accounts of many events reveals that God invites us

3. Blomberg, C. 1987. *The Historical Reliabiblity
of the Gospels*. Intervarsity. p12-35.

to explore writings that He controls under conditions in which inerrancy is humanly impossible, four different independent mindsets in human writers. This shows us gospel inerrancy we observe in our study is entirely God's work. Four identical gospels would serve no purpose and would suggest copying, but four independent perfectly-correlated gospels magnify the glory of Christ, the ultimate scripture writer (and defeat scholar-skeptics).

Differences in John's gospel: It's useful to contrast John's gospel and the synoptics. John is different from the synoptics, some points of doctrine and information being seen only in John. The fact of some items exclusive to this gospel further emphasizes independence of the writers, despite their common message. John was closest to Christ in love and faith and was chosen to illustrate independence most pointedly, likely to show us God stresses individuality (a herd mentality promotes acceptance of error). John was chosen to emphasize Christ's deity, as expected for one closer in faith, and this distinguishes his gospel.

Scholar-skeptics are suspicious of the reliability of John's gospel on the grounds that his words in the text sometimes seem to blend seamlessly with the words of Jesus, suggesting to them some kind of fraud. This observation of skeptics is questionable but, if true, would be no surprise to those who believe in verbal/ plenary inspiration. God gave this gospel writer special privilege in reporting on the deity of Christ. This makes John's gospel unique in various ways, and, we may be witnessing special proof of inspiration in his writing. Perhaps John shows us inspiration in its ultimate aspect in that his words might take on resemblance to the speech of the very divinity empowering his writing. Thus scholar skepticism of this type can prove John truly is a prophet of God, reproducing God's Words precisely. This is no different from the Psalms where David, in speaking of himself, at times moves seamlessly into speaking future words of Christ, the Son of David. For example, in Psalm 69 up to verse 20, David speaks of his reproach by his enemies, and in verse 21, there is a clear seamless transition to the words of the Savior concerning His reproach and the offering to Him of gall and vinegar on the Cross. The gall and vinegar would be only symbolic of David's experience with his enemies, but they were literal aspects of Christ's experience with His enemies.

Two unique items: In concluding this section, it is appropriate to address two particularly notable differences between John's gospel and the synoptics that many scholars say are contradictions. One is a difference in the hour of Christ's Crucifixion in John's gospel by contrast with the synoptics, and this matter was shown to be anything but a contradiction in the discussion beginning on page 50 of the present book. The other matter is a supposed different chronology of Christ's cleansing of the temple, this event occurring early in chapter 2 in John's gospel, in contrast with the accounts in the synoptics where it occurs in final days of Christ's earthly ministry. It's appropriate to discuss the temple cleansing here to further point out how misguided scholar skepticism is concerning inerrancy of scripture.

There's no random confusion among gospel writers as to the time of temple cleansing (or the hour of Crucifixion). Rather, only John's gospel is different, which is meant to show that special illumination was given to this writer. John's gospel deals with the final days of Christ's earthly ministry much more extensively than the synoptics, this being a main subject covered throughout chapters 11-21. And Christ's final earthly days that center on His death on the Cross, are emphasized very early in John's gospel in chapter 2 in the turning of water into wine at a wedding in Cana. The wine relates to Jesus' death, as we see in His response to Mary's request for wine, telling her His hour (Crucifixion) isn't yet come (the wine symbolizes His blood). In chapter 3 He emphasizes the lifting-up of the Son of Man to Nicodemus as He speaks of how the brazen serpent of Moses is symbolic of His own Crucifixion. In chapter 5, the wrath of the Jews against Him for healing on the Sabbath emphasizes His coming appointment with the Cross, and here He also speaks of the death and resurrection of mankind in a manner that associates it with His own death and Resurrection. In chapter 6, He gives a lengthy discourse related to His death on the Cross as He speaks of eating His flesh and drinking His blood (in a spiritual sense) to the Jews, and He also speaks of the future betrayal by Judas. Chapter 7 begins with a note on the danger of walking among the Jews since they already seek to kill Him, and He also speaks of giving of the Spirit that will follow His death. Chapter 8 deals with an account of Jews who try to deliver Christ to authorities by trying to trap Him in His words regarding the woman taken in adultery, and here He also notes His coming crucifixion in verses 20-28. Chapter 9 deals with His Sabbath-day healing of a blind man that enrages the Jews and further emphasizes the Cross to come. In chapter 10 in verses 10-18, Christ notes He has come to give His life for His sheep, and later in this chapter, He again incurs the wrath of the Jews that will lead to the Cross.

Actually all chapters in John, except 1 and 4, deal with this primary emphasis of John on the final days of Christ's earthly ministry, so it's no surprise that the temple cleansing of the final days appears so early in chapter 2. The chapter deals with two events, the Cana-wine miracle and the temple cleansing, which is for the purpose of connecting the two. The connection is made, for the wine prophesies of a type of temple cleansing to come at the close of Christ's earthly ministry. The Cana wine symbolizes Christ's blood in death (Jn.2:4), and cleansing of merchandising in God's Jerusalem temple (Jn.2:13-17) symbolizes cleansing of sin merchandising in the human temple that is ordained as God's temple. Intentional correlation of the literal temple with the human one is seen in John 2:19 where Christ, standing by the Jerusalem temple, emphasizes His body, rather than the building, as God's ultimate temple. In John 2:19 Christ says that His temple body will die and be resurrected, emphasizing bearing our sin and shedding His blood in death to cleanse us of all sin merchandising and make our bodies proper temples for God's name by His Spirit to dwell in. Thus symbolic blood of the Cana wine is connected with symbolic human-temple cleansing at the Jerusalem temple, and both prophesy of the Cross.

We see that chapter 2 begins emphasis on the primary subject of John's gospel in chapters 2-21, and he simply takes the event out of normal chronological order to emphasize his primary subject early. Throughout his gospel he fills in details of matters regarding his main emphasis and inserts other aspects of Christ's earthly ministry of significance for his account. None of this is in any way indicative of contradiction or error but is simply the writing style John is providentially permitted to use.

Indeed John's style here is like his style in the Revelation, where he places things out of chronological order several times for the sake of emphasizing certain concepts at crucial points in the book. For example, Revelation 12 gives a brief summary of the history of Israel, the church and Satan that cannot possibly appear in the chronological order of the book, but is crucial to the theme he presents at this point. John exhibits a concern for topical order in preference to chronological order. As Augustine noted long ago, this is characteristic of scripture, for there are some aspects of emphasis in scripture far more important than observing chronological order.

In summary, a similar gospel message with differences in specifics shows why there are four gospels, to reveal divine authorship in control of independent human writers. Of course there are four also since Christ is scripture's main personage, and four is little enough to devote to Him. True Christians should see that scholars who devised source criticism were just skeptics with a predetermined agenda aimed only at supporting their skepticism.

Form criticism: This higher-criticism method would categorize scripture according to form, or genre, and life-setting. It's based on an assumption that much of the Old and New Testaments was passed on orally before being written and that much scripture grew out of the life of the people in their links to other cultures.[4] This concept lowers the standard of scripture inspiration greatly, suggesting all kinds of error arising from frailties of mankind. The tradition would eventually be recorded, but there would be no basis to presume this written material of human origin would constitute God's true Word. It would be as if men rather than God determined scripture content and context. The only proper position regarding human tradition is to view God as using historical human events in His own composition of the Word. This is very logical since scripture shows us God dealing with mankind on the basis of historical failure and success.

Scholars think they see a validity for form criticism in pagan traditions of non-Hebrew cultures that have some resemblance to scriptural accounts, suggesting a common oral human tradition for the writings. There are some similarities of Hebrew scriptural accounts and aspects of non-Hebrew culture, as in the case of the Great Flood, but that doesn't mean scripture shares aspects of pagan culture. Similarities in flood tradition are expected since all inhabitants of the world descended from the occupants of the ark, and all had some basic knowledge of the flood event. This knowledge would become distorted in tales of various religions originating in descendents of Ham and Japheth, while Hebrew descendants of Shem retained a true authorized account of God's works record-ed in scripture. Or else God gave scripture penmen a true account because accuracy had deteriorated among all civilizations. Either way, the technical and historical superiority of the narratives of scripture is accounted for.

There is also some similarity of Moses' law to the law code of the Babylonian ruler Hammurabi, but that doesn't mean Mosaic law was influenced by the Hammurabi code. Again, we note all civilizations derived from ark survivors, and some commonality of social and political life is likely. In this regard, we need to

---

4. Johnson, Ibid.

realize that God's law didn't suddenly appear at Mount Sinai but began in the garden with Adam and the prohibition of eating certain fruit. The law began to develop after Cain slew Abel, long before Hammurabi's time. Likely there was some transfer of culture and law from descendants of Shem to others, and eventually to the Babylonians. But, apart from the common ark-survivor origin, some similarity is expected just as a result of the commonality in the social estate of man that requires obvious common solutions, and in this regard, we should ask how many logical solutions there are to each human problem.

"Criticizing" Scholar Criticism of Scripture

Criticizing source criticism

Basics: This suggests scripture's source is man's history accounts. Supposedly Pentateuch 3rd person statements like, *The Lord spake unto Moses,* reveal text content by an unknown writer. But Moses likely wrote parts of the Pentateuch, and dictated parts to an associate. The author was Moses, but at times the writing was that of another, as with Paul's epistles. Indeed Pentateuch common 3rd-person use reveals that the writer doesn't dare to misrepresent sacred truth.

Now the associate didn't just take dictation, but wrote what Moses could not write or dictate, such as, *the man Moses was very meek, above all the men...upon the face of the earth* (Num. 12:3), and he wrote about Moses' death (Dt.34). The Spirit dictates to Moses, but an associate recording scripture is a God-ordained extension of the prophet's voice, sharing in the Spirit's direction of Moses and adding inerrant notes. This reflects the gospel of Mark, who wasn't an apostle, but was an associate of the apostle and scripture-penman Peter. The association and Mark's sharing in the Spirit's direction of Peter in writing would be a basis for Mark's gospel (Mark's writing was even said to interpret Peter).

110

Documentary hypothesis: This denies Mosaic authorship of the Pentateuch, attributing it to four sources in history centuries after Moses. It suggests Pentateuch credibility is nil and the history of Israel's God and the patriarchs are an invention. Studies show the theory is based on poor scholarship misrepresenting scripture. It was once highly regarded, but its error is increasingly exposed by archaeological studies agreeing with Pentateuch historical data on laws, names, customs, etc. for appropriate times in history. The facts support Mosaic authorship and chronology and refute the theory. Writers in late times that are postulated in the theory could not possibly have a close familiarity with very early data seen in the Pentateuch and verified by archaeological studies.[5,6,7]

Interpretation error: Source-criticism scholarship superficiality is seen in its proposal that Genesis 1 and 2 originate in two different sources with two discordant creation accounts. Chapter 1 gives a broad view of creation, and chapter two a specific view focusing on man and his local environment, which is a normal literary device.

Other alleged discordant double references are a supposed twice naming of Bethel by Jacob (Gen.28:19,35:15) and twice changing of Jacob's name to Israel (Gen.32:28,35:10), which are not double references, but accounts of related different, matters.

In Gen.28:19 Jacob is in a place where he encounters God. The text says, *he called* the name of that place Bethel: *but the name of that city was called Luz* at the first, contrasting the names. In 35:15, years later, he's in distress over a <u>different </u>matter, killing of some men by his sons, and he returns to Bethel, again seeking God's guidance. In both verses, locals call the town Luz, and 35:6 says, *Luz...that is Bethel*, relating the two names to one town. In 35:15 Jacob didn't name the town a first time but just

<u>5</u> Davis Dictionary of the Bible. 1973. Royal. p621.
<u>6</u>.Thompson, J.A. 1962. *The Bible and Archaeology*. Eerdemans. p70,71.
<u>7</u>.McDowell, J.1979. *Evid. that Demands a Verdict*. V.1. Nelson. p68-70.

reaffirmed a name that hadn't yet taken hold but would one day. Bethel, House of God, is what the place was to Jacob, but it was still Luz to the locals.

In Gen.32:28 an angel says Jacob *shall be called no more Jacob, but Israel,* speaking of a future promise. The fulfillment is in Gen.35:10 that says, *Thy name is Jacob* (It's still Jacob but is about to change to fulfill the promise) *thy name shall not be called any more Jacob, but Israel shall be thy name: and he called his name Israel* (the change occurred once, at this time).

Ewert further shows how precarious interpretation of critics can be, even when they favor a true reading, as at 1 Cor.15:51 where Paul says, *We shall not all sleep, but we shall all be changed.* Ewert says this is a true, but difficult, reading since Paul did die. But Paul wasn't speaking of himself or his peers as not dying, but of those alive at the Rapture, for *we* are the saved of all ages. The reading is logical, and for modern scholars to say it explains the origin of a series of distorted related readings in other texts is misleading, suggesting the true reading began corruption seen in other texts (which assists acceptance of Alexandrian-text error), when its orthodoxy reveals corruptions seen elsewhere. The tenet is a useless device rightly discarded and replaced by the simple recognition of attempts to corrupt orthodox readings.[8]

A so-called Synoptic Problem: New Testament source criticism addresses relationships among the three synoptic gospels. Much of Mark's shorter gospel is similar to Matthew's and Luke's, so critics say Mark wrote first and Luke and Matthew copied from him, adding things, or Mark edited Matthew and Luke accounts. They can't even tell which gospel is first and are just speculating. Events in Matthew and Luke, together or separately, aren't in Mark, so critics invent other sources, one being common to the two writers.

8. Ewert, D. 1983. *From Ancient Tablets to Modern Translations.* Zondervan. p160

The synoptics show similarities in verbatim wording and non-chronological ordering of events unexpected of independent writers, but this shows God's control of independent writers. Mark's shorter gospel shows his independence, and more detail in Matthew/Luke complete the common message and reveal their independence; a good example is different aspects of Christmas accounts in Luke and Matthew. The differences fit perfectly into the overall account, and three gospels with parallel accounts reveal God's inerrancy given under humanly-impossible conditions of three different mindsets. Four identical gospels would serve no purpose, but perfectly-correlated independent gospels glorify Christ, the true author.

Proving gospel accuracy: John's gospel is said to conflict with the Synoptic in that Jesus' temple cleansing occurs early in His ministry in John 2, but late in final days of ministry in the synoptics. But there is no gospel confusion on the time of temple cleansing. John relates final days of Jesus' ministry (especially in ch.11-21) far more extensively than the synoptics do, and final earthly days centered on the Cross are stressed very early in John 2 in turning water to wine at Cana. The wine signifies His shed blood, as seen in His reply to Mary's request for wine, saying His hour (the Cross) isn't yet come. In chapter 3 He speaks of lifting-up of the Son of Man in saying Moses' brazen serpent on a pole signifies His Cross. In chapter 5, the Jews are angered by His Sabbath-day healing, emphasizing the coming Cross, and here He notes the death and resurrection of mankind that relates to His own death and Resurrection. In chapter 6 He speaks much of His death in talking to the Jews of eating His flesh and drinking His blood (in a spiritual sense) and tells of future betrayal by Judas. Chapter 7 notes the danger of walking among the Jews since they already seek to kill Him, and He tells of giving of the Spirit following His death. Chapter 8 deals with Jews trying to trap Him in His words over an adulterous woman, and here He tells of the Cross in verses 20-28. Chapter 9 notes His Sabbath-day healing of a blind man enraging the Jews, again emphasizing the Cross. In verses 10:10-18, He says He's come to give His life for His sheep, and He again stirs up the Jews' wrath leading to the Cross.

All chapters in John but 1 and 4 relate John's main emphasis on final days of Christ's earthly ministry, so it's no surprise that temple cleansing of final days appears early in chapter 2. Two events are noted here, the Cana-wine miracle and temple cleansing, connecting the two. Wine signifying His shed blood (Jn.2:4) relates to cleansing of the Jerusalem temple. Temple cleansing of merchandising (Jn.2:13-17) relates to Christ's blood cleansing us of human-temple sin-merchandising at the close of His earthly ministry. John 2:19 correlates the literal and human temples as Jesus, near the Jerusalem temple, emphasizes His body, not the building, as God's temple. In John 2:19 He reveals that His temple body will die and will be resurrected, thus emphasizing bearing our sin and shedding His blood to cleanse us of sin merchandising and make our bodies temples for God's name by His Spirit to dwell in. Thus Cana-wine symbolic blood relates to symbolic human-temple cleansing at the Jerusalem temple, and both relate to the Cross.

Chapter 2 begins emphasis on John's main subject. He simply takes it out of chronological order for emphasis. This isn't error, but John's permitted writing style, as seen in Revelation as he sets aside chronological order to emphasize concepts at crucial places. For example Revelation 12 briefly summarizes the history of Israel, the church and Satan that can't be in chronological order but is vital to the theme he presents at this point. John stresses the more important topical order in preference to the chronological.

For all who desire to live their lives focused on truth, the credibility of modern scholars in attacking and discrediting the traditional texts of scripture text is nil. The traditional Bible-language text is God's inerrant Word preserved from the autographs, and the KJV is the one English translation that continues complete preservation.

Appendix B

Dating of Job: Job was written ~2000 B.C, preceding the Pentateuch, for it doesn't mention Israel, and it shows the man Job personally administering the animal sacrifice of Abel and Noah, preceding a priestly-administered one of Moses. It says nothing of Abraham, greatest figure of his time, and Job was, *greatest of all the men of the east* (1:3), so the book was likely written before Abraham's time, ~2000 B.C. The name Uz, Job's land, is very old, dating to Noah's great-grandson (Gen.10:21-23). Job preceded Abraham, Job's life span being the 140 years he lived after his trials (42:16), plus preceding years in which he grew to manhood and begat 10 children old enough to sin (1:1-5), for a likely total of ~200 years. This is close to the 205 years of Abraham's father, Terah, and greater than the 175 of Abraham, the 147 of Jacob and the 110 of Jacob's son Joseph. This places Job close to Terah as the life-span decreased from a near-1000 year pre-flood level.

Another indicator that Job is first is its description of ancient dinosaurs. And logic places Job first, for it deals with the foremost human dilemma, the question of why hurt and evil dominate life, and it presents the answer, the Savior (Job 19:25-27).

Now we must account for links of names of Chaldean and Sabean tribes and the tribe of the friend Elihu to descendants of Abraham and Nahor. The name *Chaldean* preceded Abraham's time, for his first homeland was Ur of the Chaldees (Gen.11:31), and *Sabean* originated with Seba, Noah's great grandson (Gen.10:1-7). And the Naamathite tribal name of Job's friend Zophar, originated with the name of Cain's great granddaughter (Gen.4:22). Thus the links likely are later repeat uses of very early names.

We must also account for Job's friends Eliphaz and Bildad having personal and/or tribal names identified with descendants of Abraham (Esau, Shuah, Jokshan - Gen.25:2) and his brother Nahor (Gen.22:20,21). Inexact genealogy correlation indicates names in descent lines of Abraham and Nahor are repeat uses of names in Job. For example Eliphaz in Job is called a Temanite, while 1 Chron.1:36 says Teman in Abraham's line was a son of Eliphaz; a father can't continue a clan of which his son is patriarch, so Eliphaz in Abraham's line is a different Eliphaz. And Elihu the <u>Buz</u>ite of Job has a father Barachel not noted in the line of Nahor, father of <u>Buz</u> and Huz (Gen.22:21), and Job's Ram in the line of Buz isn't in Nahor's line, the one other Ram in the Bible being in Abraham's line (1 Chron.2:9 - Aram in Nahor's line and Ram are different names). And Nahor's Huz and Buz are names likely derived from Job's land Uz, reflecting a trend in Nahor's clan in that his name derived from the name of his town and his brother Haran's from the district of the town of Nahor. Job could be a son of Jacob's son Issachar (Gen.46:13), placing him around 1800-1700 B.C, but this is likely another use of *Job*, for nothing ties this man to Job's greatness in the Job book.

Repeat use of names in descent lines of Job and friends, in similar order, is no surprise. Children have long been named for Bible figures. As Abraham was the greatest man in his age, Job was in his, and children would be named after names in Job, this being the only Bible book at Abraham's time and for the next 500 years. Similar order likely reflects honoring of the first Bible book, and descendants of Abraham and Nahor would likely want their children's names to reflect the Job book due to great faith in God common to Job and Abraham. Inaccuracy in repeating names in a line would be due to conflicting human preferences, limited Bible-text availability so early in history and uncertain early record-keeping. Record-keeping evidently began with the book of Numbers and developed further in Chronicles, Ezra and Nehemiah.

Appendix C

Illustrating Why Old English is Rightly Retained.
(Defining older words in a glossary is appropriate)

Exodus 20:13 (and Deuteronomy 5:17).

KJB: *Thou shalt not kill*
NIV: *You shall not murder*
NASV: *You shall not murder*
NKJV: *You shall not murder*

1.*Thou* is a singular pronoun (the Hebrew is singular), so it refers to the individual. It tells him he can't decide to end life, for that's God's prerogative. Ending life by a personal decision includes an act like abortion, but *murder* doesn't. Individuals have no right to abortion anymore than to murder, yet often violate this law, not even knowing it's a sin if they use only a modern version.

God permits government to kill in just warfare or punishment of capital crime (Rom.13:1-5). If *thou* in the correct KJB reading were replaced by singular or plural *you*, that applies corporately or individually, it would forbid government to do its duty.

2. *Ye* is plural, and this distinction is lost in the modern *you*.

3. *Ensample* refers to a sample of the real thing, while *example* is usually just an approximation of the real thing.

4. *Astonied* refers to a degree of surprise leaving one speechless and unable to react (stone-like), while *astonished* often refers to surprise of a lesser degree

5. *Throughly* refers to *through and through*, a maximal degree of thoroughness, while *thorough* can be of lesser degree.

6. *Trespass* confers a dreaded sense of being off-limits on God's will, in addition to the sense of breaking God's law by *sin*.

7. *Husbandman* conveys the image of a man who takes care of the land rather than just using it to his purposes.

8. *Translate* includes a necessary change of state for living in God's kingdom, and thus is superior to *transfer*.

9. *Apparently*, meaning *openly*, has deteriorated to *seemingly*.

10. *Quick* means *alive*, and the intent is activity vs. deadness.
11. *Carefulness* means *full of cares*, and being free of this is more basic to the faith than the modern sense of *caution*.
12. *Prevent* means *go before*, relating to our faith in God who goes before us on our way, a sense more important than *stop*.
13. *Mansion*, a dwelling place that can be huge, offers different-iation from *room* that can signify a small seating place.
14. *Reins* (lit. *kidneys*) means *mind* and signifies crucial control.
15. *Vanities* or *deceptions* reveals vanity as the source of deceit.
16. *Wrest* for *twist* imparts a sense of wrestling with conscience.
17. *Veil* includes the purpose, as well as the form, of *curtain*.
18. *Strait* adds to *narrow* (obedience or doctrine), a true sense of restricted direction, as well as breadth, as in a seawater strait.
19. *Charity* refers to divine sacrificial love and covers all aspects of it, which is far more significant than *love*, which can be as insignificant as love of sports or love of certain foods.
20. *Base* is more precise than *lowly*, referring to the most basic or foundational aspect of something that is of low character.
21. *Beggarly* is more intensive in sense than *worthless*, suggest-ing an ultimate end of dependence on others for basic needs.
22. *Castaway* reflects the emotional grievous result of *rejected.*
23. *Chambering* reflects the common locale of *sensual living* and emphasizes the error of such matters.
24. *Draught* is a term more suited to the sacred text than *sewer*.
25. *Conversant*, the sense of *at home with*, is still widely used, as in the case of being conversant with technical matters.
26. *Cubit*, the distance from elbow to finger-tip is a convenient rough measure requiring no equipment.
27. *Diviner*, imitator of God's power, reveals the depth of error.
28. *Earnest* rightly signifies the nature of true *security*.
29. *Horn*, as a mountain or tusk, is an emphatic *power symbol*
30. *Instant* communicates the timing of *urgent*.
31. *Latchet* conveys the image of latching, fastening of a *thong*.
32. *Listeth* conveys an image of listing to one side in *choosing*

Made in the USA
Charleston, SC
17 July 2012